ABOUT THIS PUBLICATION

FOR SERVICE ASSISTANCE

Customer Service Department
704.898.0770

North Carolina General Statues is published by The Muliti-Media Group of Greater Charlotte in Charlotte, North Carolina. Copyright 2015 by the Multi-Media Group of Greater Charlotte. This book or parts thereof may not be reproduced in any form, stored in a retrieval system, or transmitted in any form by any means—electronic, mechanical, photocopy, recording or otherwise—without prior written permission of the publisher, except as provided by United States of America copyright law.

The records required by U.S. Code 2257(a) through (c) and the pertinent regulations 28 C.F.R. Cli. 1, Part 75 with respect to this publication and all materials associated with such records are maintained by The Multi-Media Group of Greater Charlotte, Publisher and available for review by Attorney General.

www.visionbooks.org

Copyright © 2015 by MMGGC
All rights reserved!

TID: 4989448
ISBN (10) digit: 1502305798
ISBN (13) digit: 978-1502305794

123-4-56789-01239-Paperback
123-4-56789-01239-Hardback

First Edition

090520140547

Printed in the United States of America

2015 EDITION

North Carolina Criminal Law And Procedure-Pamphlet # 6

Printed In conjunction with the Administration of the Courts

North Carolina Criminal Law and Procedure
Pamphlet Reference Guide

Chapters	Pamphlet
Chapter 1 Civil Procedure	1
Chapter 1 Civil Procedure (Continue)	2
Chapter 1A Rules of Civil Procedure	2
Chapter 1B Contribution.	2
Chapter 1C Enforcement of Judgments.	2
Chapter 1D Punitive Damages.	2
Chapter 1E Eastern Band of Cherokee Indians.	2
Chapter 1F North Carolina Uniform Interstate Depositions and Discovery Act.	2
Chapter 2 - Clerk of Superior Court [Repealed and Transferred.]	3
Chapter 3 - Commissioners of Affidavits and Deeds [Repealed.]	3
Chapter 4 - Common Law	3
Chapter 5 - Contempt [Repealed.]	3
Chapter 5A - Contempt	3
Chapter 6 - Liability for Court Costs	3
Chapter 7 - Courts [Repealed and Transferred.]	3
Chapter 7A – Judicial Department	3
Chapter 7A – Continuation (Judicial Department)	4
Chapter 7A – Continuation (Judicial Department)	5
Chapter 7B - Juvenile Code	5
Chapter 8 - Evidence	6
Chapter 8A - Interpreters for Deaf Persons [Recodified.]	6
Chapter 8B - Interpreters for Deaf Persons	6
Chapter 8C - Evidence Code	6
Chapter 9 - Jurors	6
Chapter 10 - Notaries [Repealed.]	6
Chapter 10A - Notaries [Recodified.]	6
Chapter 10B - Notaries	6
Chapter 11 - Oaths	6
Chapter 12 - Statutory Construction	6
Chapter 13 - Citizenship Restored	6
Chapter 14 - Criminal Law	7
Chapter 14 –Criminal Law (Continuation)	8
Chapter 15 - Criminal Procedure	9
Chapter 15A - Criminal Procedure Act (Continuation)	10
Chapter 15A - Criminal Procedure Act (Continuation)	11
Chapter 15B - Victims Compensation	11
Chapter 15C - Address Confidentiality Program	11
Chapter 16 - Gaming Contracts and Futures	11
Chapter 17 - Habeas Corpus	11

Chapter 17A - Law-Enforcement Officers [Recodified.]	11
Chapter 17B - North Carolina Criminal Justice Education and Training System [Recodified.] Chapter 17C - North Carolina Criminal Justice Education and Training Standards Commission	11 11
Chapter 17D - North Carolina Justice Academy	11
Chapter 17E - North Carolina Sheriffs' Education and Training Standards Commission	11
Chapter 18 - Regulation of Intoxicating Liquors [Repealed.]	12
Chapter 18A - Regulation of Intoxicating Liquors [Repealed.]	12
Chapter 18B - Regulation of Alcoholic Beverages	12
Chapter 18C - North Carolina State Lottery	12
Chapter 19 - Offenses against Public Morals	12
Chapter 19A - Protection of Animals	12
Chapter 20 - Motor Vehicles	13
Chapter 20 - Motor Vehicles (Continuation)	14
Chapter 20 - Motor Vehicles (Continuation)	15
Chapter 20 - Motor Vehicles (Continuation)	16
Chapter 21 - Bills of Lading	17
Chapter 22 - Contracts Requiring Writing	17
Chapter 22A - Signatures	17
Chapter 22B - Contracts Against Public Policy	17
Chapter 22C - Payments to Subcontractors	17
Chapter 23 - Debtor and Creditor	17
Chapter 24 – Interest	17
Chapter 25 – Uniform Commercial Code	18
Chapter 25 – Uniform Commercial Code (Continuation)	19
Chapter 25A – Retail Installment Sales Act	20
Chapter 25B - Credit	20
Chapter 25C - Sales of Artwork	20
Chapter 26 - Suretyship	20
Chapter 27 - Warehouse Receipts [Repealed.]	20
Chapter 28 - Administration [Repealed.]	20
Chapter 28A - Administration of Decedents' Estates	20
Chapter 28B - Estates of Absentees in Military Service	20
Chapter 28C - Estates of Missing Persons	20
Chapter 29 - Intestate Succession	21
Chapter 30 - Surviving Spouses	21
Chapter 31 - Wills	21
Chapter 31A - Acts Barring Property Rights	21
Chapter 31B - Renunciation of Property and Renunciation of Fiduciary Powers Act	21
Chapter 31C - Uniform Disposition of Community Property Rights at Death Act	21
Chapter 32 - Fiduciaries	21
Chapter 32A - Powers of Attorney	21
Chapter 33 - Guardian and Ward [Repealed and Recodified.]	21

Chapter 33A - North Carolina Uniform Transfers to Minors Act	21
Chapter 33B - North Carolina Uniform Custodial Trust Act	21
Chapter 34 - Veterans' Guardianship Act	22
Chapter 35 - Sterilization Procedures	22
Chapter 35A - Incompetency and Guardianship	22
Chapter 36 - Trusts and Trustees [Repealed.]	22
Chapter 36A - Trusts and Trustees	22
Chapter 36B - Uniform Management of Institutional Funds Act [Repealed.]	22
Chapter 36C - North Carolina Uniform Trust Code	22
Chapter 36D - North Carolina Community Third Party Trusts, Pooled Trusts	23
Chapter 36E - Uniform Prudent Management of Institutional Funds Act	23
Chapter 37 - Allocation of Principal and Income [Repealed.]	23
Chapter 37A - Uniform Principal and Income Act	23
Chapter 38 - Boundaries	23
Chapter 38A - Landowner Liability	23
Chapter 39 - Conveyances	23
Chapter 39A - Transfer Fee Covenants Prohibited	23
Chapter 40 - Eminent Domain [Repealed.]	23
Chapter 40A - Eminent Domain	23
Chapter 41 - Estates	23
Chapter 41A - State Fair Housing Act	23
Chapter 42 - Landlord and Tenant	23
Chapter 42A - Vacation Rental Act	23
Chapter 43 - Land Registration	23
Chapter 44 - Liens	24
Chapter 44A - Statutory Liens and Charges	24
Chapter 45 - Mortgages and Deeds of Trust	24
Chapter 45A - Good Funds Settlement Act	24
Chapter 46 - Partition	24
Chapter 47 - Probate and Registration	25
Chapter 47A - Unit Ownership	25
Chapter 47B - Real Property Marketable Title Act	25
Chapter 47C - North Carolina Condominium Act	25
Chapter 47D - Notice of Settlement Act [Expired.]	25
Chapter 47E - Residential Property Disclosure Act	25
Chapter 47F - North Carolina Planned Community Act	25
Chapter 47G - Option to Purchase Contracts	25
Chapter 47H - Contracts for Deed	25
Chapter 48 – Adoptions	26
Chapter 48A - Minors	26
Chapter 49 - Bastardy	26
Chapter 49A - Rights of Children	26
Chapter 50 - Divorce and Alimony	26
Chapter 50A - Uniform Child-Custody Jurisdiction and	

Enforcement Act	26
Chapter 50B - Domestic Violence	26
Chapter 50C - Civil No-Contact Orders	26
Chapter 51 - Marriage	26
Chapter 52 - Powers and Liabilities of Married Persons	27
Chapter 52A - Uniform Reciprocal Enforcement of Support Act [Repealed.]	27
Chapter 52B - Uniform Premarital Agreement Act	27
Chapter 52C - Uniform Interstate Family Support Act	27
Chapter 53 - Banks	27
Chapter 53A - Business Development Corporations and North Carolina Capital Resource Corporations	28
Chapter 53B - Financial Privacy Act	28
Chapter 54 - Cooperative Organizations	28
Chapter 54A - Capital Stock Savings and Loan Associations [Repealed.]	28
Chapter 54B - Savings and Loan Associations	29
Chapter 54C - Savings Banks	29
Chapter 55 - North Carolina Business Corporation Act	30
Chapter 55A - North Carolina Nonprofit Corporation Act	31
Chapter 55B - Professional Corporation Act	31
Chapter 55C - Foreign Trade Zones	31
Chapter 55D - Filings, Names, and Registered Agents for Corporations, Nonprofit Corporations, and Partnerships	31
Chapter 56 - Electric, Telegraph and Power Companies [Repealed.]	31
Chapter 57 - Hospital, Medical and Dental Service Corporations [Recodified.]	31
Chapter 57A - Health Maintenance Organization Act [Recodified.]	31
Chapter 57B - Health Maintenance Organization Act [Recodified.]	31
Chapter 57C - North Carolina Limited Liability Company Act.	31
Chapter 58 - Insurance.	32
Chapter 58 - Insurance (Continuation)	33
Chapter 58 - Insurance (Continuation)	34
Chapter 58 - Insurance (Continuation)	35
Chapter 58 - Insurance (Continuation)	36
Chapter 58 - Insurance (Continuation)	37
Chapter 58 - Insurance (Continuation)	38
Chapter 58A - North Carolina Health Insurance Trust Commission [Recodified.]	38
Chapter 59 - Partnership.	39
Chapter 59B - Uniform Unincorporated Nonprofit Association Act.	39
Chapter 60 - Railroads and Other Carriers [Repealed and Transferred.]	39
Chapter 61 - Religious Societies	39
Chapter 62 - Public Utilities	39

Chapter 62 - Public Utilities (Continuation)	40
Chapter 62A - Public Safety Telephone Service And Wireless Telephone Service	40
Chapter 63 - Aeronautics	40
Chapter 63A - North Carolina Global TransPark Authority	40
Chapter 64 - Aliens	40
Chapter 65 – Cemeteries	40
Chapter 66 - Commerce and Business	41
Chapter 67 - Dogs	41
Chapter 68 - Fences and Stock Law	41
Chapter 69 - Fire Protection	41
Chapter 70 - Indian Antiquities, Archaeological Resources and Unmarked Human Skeletal Remains Protection	42
Chapter 71 - Indians [Repealed.]	42
Chapter 71A - Indians	42
Chapter 72 - Inns, Hotels and Restaurants	42
Chapter 73 - Mills	42
Chapter 74 - Mines and Quarries	42
Chapter 74A - Company Police [Repealed.]	42
Chapter 74B - Private Protective Services Act [Repealed.]	42
Chapter 74C - Private Protective Services	42
Chapter 74D - Alarm Systems	42
Chapter 74E - Company Police Act	42
Chapter 74F - Locksmith Licensing Act	42
Chapter 74G - Campus Police Act	42
Chapter 75 - Monopolies, Trusts and Consumer Protection	42
Chapter 75A - Boating and Water Safety	43
Chapter 75B - Discrimination in Business	43
Chapter 75C - Motion Picture Fair Competition Act	43
Chapter 75D - Racketeer Influenced and Corrupt Organizations	43
Chapter 75E - Unlawful Activities in Connection With Certain Corporate Transactions	43
Chapter 76 - Navigation	43
Chapter 76A - Navigation and Pilotage Commissions	43
Chapter 77 - Rivers, Creeks, and Coastal Waters	43
Chapter 78 - Securities Law [Repealed.]	43
Chapter 78A - North Carolina Securities Act	43
Chapter 78B - Tender Offer Disclosure Act [Repealed.]	43
Chapter 78C - Investment Advisers	43
Chapter 78D - Commodities Act	43
Chapter 79 - Strays [Repealed.]	43
Chapter 80 - Trademarks, Brands, etc.	44
Chapter 81 - Weights and Measures [Recodified.]	44
Chapter 81A - Weights and Measures Act of 1975.	44
Chapter 82 - Wrecks [Repealed.]	44
Chapter 83 - Architects [Recodified.]	44

Chapter 83A - Architects	44
Chapter 84 - Attorneys-at-Law	44
Chapter 84A - Foreign Legal Consultants	44
Chapter 85 - Auctions and Auctioneers [Repealed.]	44
Chapter 85A - Bail Bondsmen and Runners [Recodified.]	44
Chapter 85B - Auctions and Auctioneers	44
Chapter 85C - Bail Bondsmen and Runners [Recodified.]	44
Chapter 86 - Barbers [Recodified.]	44
Chapter 86A - Barbers	44
Chapter 87 - Contractors	44
Chapter 88 - Cosmetic Art [Repealed.]	44
Chapter 88A - Electrolysis Practice Act	44
Chapter 88B - Cosmetic Art	45
Chapter 89 - Engineering and Land Surveying [Recodified.]	45
Chapter 89A - Landscape Architects	45
Chapter 89B - Foresters	45
Chapter 89C - Engineering and Land Surveying	45
Chapter 89D - Landscape Contractors	45
Chapter 89E - Geologists Licensing Act	45
Chapter 89F - North Carolina Soil Scientist Licensing Act	45
Chapter 89G - Irrigation Contractors	45
Chapter 90 - Medicine and Allied Occupations	45
Chapter 90 - Medicine and Allied Occupations (Continuation)	46
Chapter 90 - Medicine and Allied Occupations (Continuation)	47
Chapter 90 - Medicine and Allied Occupations (Continuation)	48
Chapter 90A - Sanitarians and Water and Wastewater Treatment Facility Operators	48
Chapter 90B - Social Worker Certification and Licensure Act	48
Chapter 90C - North Carolina Recreational Therapy Licensure Act	48
Chapter 90D - Interpreters and Transliterators	48
Chapter 91 - Pawnbrokers [Repealed.]	48
Chapter 91A - Pawnbrokers Modernization Act of 1989	48
Chapter 92 - Photographers [Deleted.]	48
Chapter 93 - Certified Public Accountants	48
Chapter 93A - Real Estate License Law	49
Chapter 93B - Occupational Licensing Boards	49
Chapter 93C - Watchmakers [Repealed.]	49
Chapter 93D - North Carolina State Hearing Aid Dealers and Fitters Board.	49
Chapter 93E - North Carolina Appraisers Act	49
Chapter 94 - Apprenticeship	49
Chapter 95 - Department of Labor and Labor Regulations	49
Chapter 95 - Department of Labor and Labor Regulations (Continuation)	50
Chapter 96 - Employment Security	50
Chapter 97 - Workers' Compensation Act	50
Chapter 97 - Workers' Compensation Act (Continuation)	51

Chapter 98 - Burnt and Lost Records	51
Chapter 99 - Libel and Slander	51
Chapter 99A - Civil Remedies for Criminal Actions	51
Chapter 99B - Products Liability	51
Chapter 99C - Actions Relating to Winter Sports Safety and Accidents	51
Chapter 99D - Civil Rights	51
Chapter 99E - Special Liability Provisions	51
Chapter 100 - Monuments, Memorials and Parks	51
Chapter 101 - Names of Persons	51
Chapter 102 - Official Survey Base	51
Chapter 103 - Sundays, Holidays and Special Days	51
Chapter 104 - United States Lands	51
Chapter 104A - Degrees of Kinship	51
Chapter 104B - Hurricanes or Other Acts of Nature	51
Chapter 104C - Atomic Energy, Radioactivity and Ionizing Radiation [Repealed and Recodified.]	51
Chapter 104D - Southern States Energy Compact	51
Chapter 104E - North Carolina Radiation Protection Act	51
Chapter 104F - Southeast Interstate Low-Level Radioactive Waste Management Compact [Repealed]	51
Chapter 104G - North Carolina Low-Level Radioactive Waste Management Authority Act of 1987 [Repealed]	51
Chapter 105 - Taxation	51
Chapter 105 - Taxation (Continuation)	52
Chapter 105 - Taxation (Continuation)	53
Chapter 105 - Taxation (Continuation)	54
Chapter 105A - Setoff Debt Collection Act	55
Chapter 105B - Defaulted Student Loan Recovery Act	55
Chapter 106 - Agriculture	55
Chapter 106 - Agriculture (Continue)	56
Chapter 106 - Agriculture (Continue)	57
Chapter 107 - Agricultural Development Districts [Repealed.]	57
Chapter 108 - Social Services [Repealed and Recodified.]	57
Chapter 108A - Social Services	57
Chapter 108B - Community Action Programs	58
Chapter 108C Medicaid and Health Choice Provider Requirements.	58
Chapter 108D Medicaid Managed Care for Behavioral Health Services.	58
Chapter 109 - Bonds [Recodified.]	58
Chapter 110 - Child Welfare	58
Chapter 111 - Aid to the Blind	58
Chapter 112 - Confederate Homes and Pensions [Repealed.]	58
Chapter 113 - Conservation and Development	58
Chapter 113 - Conservation and Development (Continuation)	59

Chapter 113A - Pollution Control and Environment	59
Chapter 113A - Pollution Control and Environment (Continuation)	60
Chapter 113B - North Carolina Energy Policy Act of 1975	60
Chapter 114 - Department of Justice	60
Chapter 115 - Elementary and Secondary Education [Repealed.]	60
Chapter 115A - Community Colleges, Technical Institutes, and Industrial Education Centers [Repealed.]	60
Chapter 115B - Tuition and Fee Waivers	60
Chapter 115C - Elementary and Secondary Education	60
Chapter 115C - Elementary and Secondary Education (Continuation)	61
Chapter 115C - Elementary and Secondary Education (Continuation)	62
Chapter 115C - Elementary and Secondary Education (Continuation)	63
Chapter 115D - Community Colleges	63
Chapter 115E - Private Educational Facilities Finance Act [Recodified]	63
Chapter 116 - Higher Education	63
Chapter 116 - Higher Education (Continuation)	63
Chapter 116A - Escheats and Abandoned Property [Repealed.]	64
Chapter 116B - Escheats and Abandoned Property	64
Chapter 116C - Continuum of Education Programs	64
Chapter 116D - Higher Education Bonds	64
Chapter 116E -Education Longitudinal Data System	64
Chapter 117 - Electrification	64
Chapter 118 - Firemen's and Rescue Squad Workers' Relief and Pension Funds [Recodified.]	64
Chapter 118A - Firemen's Death Benefit Act [Repealed.]	64
Chapter 118B - Members of a Rescue Squad Death Benefit Act [Repealed.]	64
Chapter 119 - Gasoline and Oil Inspection and Regulation	64
Chapter 120 - General Assembly	65
Chapter 120 - General Assembly (Continuation)	66
Chapter 120 - General Assembly (Continuation)	67
Chapter 120C - Lobbying	67
Chapter 121 - Archives and History	67
Chapter 122 - Hospitals for the Mentally Disordered [Repealed.]	67
Chapter 122A - North Carolina Housing Finance Agency	67
Chapter 122B - North Carolina Agricultural Facilities Finance Act [Repealed.]	67
Chapter 122C - Mental Health, Developmental Disabilities, and Substance Abuse Act of 1985	67
Chapter 122C - Mental Health, Developmental Disabilities, and Substance Abuse Act of 1985 (Continuation)	68

Chapter 122D - North Carolina Agricultural Finance Act	68
Chapter 122E - North Carolina Housing Trust and Oil Overcharge Act	68
Chapter 123 - Impeachment	69
Chapter 123A - Industrial Development [Repealed.]	69
Chapter 124 - Internal Improvements	69
Chapter 125 - Libraries	69
Chapter 126 - State Personnel System	69
Chapter 127 - Militia [Repealed.]	69
Chapter 127A - Militia	69
Chapter 127B - Military Affairs	69
Chapter 127C - Advisory Commission on Military Affairs	69
Chapter 128 - Offices and Public Officers	69
Chapter 128 - Offices and Public Officers (Continuation)	70
Chapter 129 - Public Buildings and Grounds	70
Chapter 130 - Public Health [Repealed.]	70
Chapter 130A - Public Health	70
Chapter 130A - Public Health (Continuation)	71
Chapter 130A - Public Health (Continuation)	72
Chapter 130B - Hazardous Waste Management Commission [Repealed.]	72
Chapter 131 - Public Hospitals [Repealed.]	72
Chapter 131A - Health Care Facilities Finance Act	72
Chapter 131B - Licensing of Ambulatory Surgical Facilities [Repealed.]	72
Chapter 131C - Charitable Solicitation Licensure Act [Repealed.]	72
Chapter 131D - Inspection and Licensing of Facilities	72
Chapter 131E - Health Care Facilities and Services	72
Chapter 131E - Health Care Facilities and Services (Continuation)	73
Chapter 131F - Solicitation of Contributions	73
Chapter 132 - Public Records	73
Chapter 133 - Public Works	74
Chapter 134 - Youth Development [Recodified.]	74
Chapter 134A - Youth Services [Repealed.]	74
Chapter 135 - Retirement System for Teachers and State Employees; Social Security; Health Insurance Program for Children	74
Chapter 135 - Retirement System for Teachers and State Employees; Social Security; Health Insurance Program for Children	75
Chapter 136 - Transportation	75
Chapter 136 - Transportation (Continuation)	76
Chapter 137 - Rural Rehabilitation [Repealed.]	76
Chapter 138 - Salaries, Fees and Allowances	76
Chapter 138A - State Government Ethics Act	76

Chapter 139 - Soil and Water Conservation Districts	76
Chapter 140 - State Art Museum; Symphony and Art Societies	76
Chapter 140A - State Awards System	76
Chapter 141 - State Boundaries	76
Chapter 142 - State Debt	76
Chapter 143 - State Departments, Institutions, and Commissions	77
Chapter 143 - State Departments, Institutions, and Commissions (Continuation)	78
Chapter 143 - State Departments, Institutions, and Commissions (Continuation)	79
Chapter 143 - State Departments, Institutions, and Commissions (Continuation)	80
Chapter 143A - State Government Reorganization	80
Chapter 143B - Executive Organization Act of 1973	80
Chapter 143B - Executive Organization Act of 1973 (Continuation)	81
Chapter 143B - Executive Organization Act of 1973 (Continuation)	82
Chapter 143C - State Budget Act	83
Chapter 143D - The State Governmental Accountability and Internal Control Act	83
Chapter 144 - State Flag, Official Governmental Flags, Motto, and Colors	83
Chapter 145 - State Symbols and Other Official Adoptions.	83
Chapter 146 - State Lands	83
Chapter 147 - State Officers	83
Chapter 148 - State Prison System	84
Chapter 149 - State Song and Toast	84
Chapter 150 - Uniform Revocation of Licenses [Repealed.]	84
Chapter 150A - Administrative Procedure Act [Recodified.]	84
Chapter 150B - Administrative Procedure Act	84
Chapter 151 - Constables [Repealed.]	84
Chapter 152 - Coroners	84
Chapter 152A - County Medical Examiner [Repealed.]	84
Chapter 152A - County Medical Examiner [Repealed.] (Continuation)	85
Chapter 153 - Counties and County Commissioners [Repealed.]	85
Chapter 153A - Counties	85
Chapter 153B - Mountain Resources Planning Act	85
Chapter 153C - Uwharrie Regional Resources Act	85
Chapter 154 - County Surveyor [Repealed.]	85
Chapter 155 - County Treasurer [Repealed.]	85
Chapter 156 - Drainage	85

Chapter 156 – Drainage (Continuation)	86
Chapter 157 - Housing Authorities and Projects	86
Chapter 157A - Historic Properties Commissions [Transferred.]	86
Chapter 158 - Local Development	86
Chapter 159 - Local Government Finance	86
Chapter 159 - Local Government Finance (Continuation)	87
Chapter 159A - Pollution Abatement and Industrial Facilities Financing Act [Unconstitutional.]	87
Chapter 159B - Joint Municipal Electric Power and Energy Act	87
Chapter 159C - Industrial and Pollution Control Facilities Financing Act	87
Chapter 159D - The North Carolina Capital Facilities Financing Act	87
Chapter 159E - Registered Public Obligations Act	87
Chapter 159F - North Carolina Energy Development Authority [Repealed.]	87
Chapter 159G - Water Infrastructure	87
Chapter 159H - [Reserved.]	87
Chapter 159I - Solid Waste Management Loan Program and Local Government Special Obligation Bonds	87
Chapter 160 - Municipal Corporations [Repealed And Transferred.]	87
Chapter 160A - Cities and Towns	88
Chapter 160A - Cities and Towns (Continuation)	89
Chapter 160B - Consolidated City-County Act	89
Chapter 160C - Baseball Park Districts [Repealed.]	90
Chapter 161 - Register of Deeds	90
Chapter 162 - Sheriff	90
Chapter 162A - Water and Sewer Systems	90
Chapter 162B Continuity of Local Government in Emergency.	90
Chapter 163 Elections and Election Laws.	90
Chapter 163 Elections and Election Laws. (Continuation)	91
Chapter 164 Concerning the General Statutes of North Carolina.	92
Chapter 165 Veterans.	92
Chapter 166 Civil Preparedness Agencies [Repealed.]	92
Chapter 166A North Carolina Emergency Management Act.	92
Chapter 167 State Civil Air Patrol [Repealed.]	92
Chapter 168 Persons with Disabilities.	92
Chapter 168A Persons With Disabilities Protection Act.	92

Chapter 8.

Evidence.

Article 1.

Statutes.

§ 8-1. Printed statutes and certified copies evidence.

All statutes, or joint resolutions, passed by the General Assembly may be read in evidence from the printed statute book; or a copy of any act of the General Assembly certified by the Secretary of State shall be received in evidence in every court. (1826, c. 7; R.C., c. 44, ss. 4, 5; Code, ss. 1339, 1340; Rev., ss. 1592, 1593; C.S., s. 1747.)

§ 8-2. Martin's collection of private acts.

Any private act published by Francis X. Martin, in his collection of private acts, shall be received in evidence in every court. (1826, c. 7, s. 2; R.C., c. 44, s. 5; Code, s. 1340; Rev., s. 1593; C.S., s. 1748.)

§ 8-3. Laws of other states or foreign countries.

(a) A printed copy of a statute, or other written law, of another state, or of a territory, or of a foreign country, or a printed copy of a proclamation, edict, decree or ordinance, by the executive thereof, contained in a book or publication purporting or proved to have been published by the authority thereof, or proved to be commonly admitted as evidence of the existing law, in the judicial tribunals thereof, shall be evidence of the statute law, proclamation, edict, decree, or ordinance. The unwritten or common law of another state, or of a territory, or of a foreign country, may be proved as a fact by oral evidence. The books of the reports of cases, adjudged in the courts thereof, shall also be admitted as evidence of the unwritten or common law thereof.

(b) Any party may exhibit a copy of the law of another state, territory, or foreign country copied from a printed volume of the laws of such state, territory, or country on file in

(1) The offices of the Governor or the Secretary of State, and duly certified by the Secretary of State, or

(2) The State Library and certified as provided in G.S. 125-6, or

(3) The Supreme Court Library and certified as provided in G.S. 7A-13 (f). (1823, c. 1193, ss. 1, 3, P.R.; R.C., c. 44, s. 3; C.C.P., s. 360; Code, s. 1338; Rev., s. 1594; C.S., s. 1749; 1967, c. 565.)

§ 8-4. Judicial notice of laws of United States, other states and foreign countries.

When any question shall arise as to the law of the United States, or of any other state or territory of the United States, or of the District of Columbia, or of any foreign country, the court shall take notice of such law in the same manner as if the question arose under the law of this State. (1931, c. 30.)

§ 8-5. Town ordinances certified.

In a trial in which the offense charged is the violation of a town ordinance, a copy of the ordinance alleged to have been violated, proven as provided in G.S. 160A-79, shall be prima facie evidence of the existence of such ordinance. (1899, c. 277, s. 2; Rev., s. 1595; C.S., s. 1750; 1971, c. 381, s. 3; 1973, c. 1446, s. 17.)

Article 2.

Grants, Deeds and Wills.

§ 8-6. Copies certified by Secretary of State or State Archivist.

Copies of the plats and certificates of survey, or their accompanying warrants, and all abstracts of grants, which may be filed in the office of the Secretary of State, or in the Department of Cultural Resources, which copies, upon certification by the Secretary of State as to those records in his office, or the State Archivist as to those records in the Department of Cultural Resources, as true copies, shall be as good evidence, in any court, as the original. (1822, c.

1154, P.R.; R.C., c. 44, s. 6; Code, s. 1341; Rev., s. 1596; C.S., s. 1751; 1961, c. 740, s. 1; 1973, c. 476, s. 48.)

§ 8-7. Certified copies of grants and abstracts.

For the purpose of showing title from the State of North Carolina to the grantee or grantees therein named and for the lands therein described, duly certified copies of all grants and of all memoranda and abstracts of grants on record in the office of the Secretary of State, or in the Department of Cultural Resources, given in abstract or in full, and with or without the signature of the Governor and the great seal of the State appearing upon such record, shall be competent evidence in the courts of this State or of the United States or of any territory of the United States, and in the absence of the production of the original grant shall be conclusive evidence of a grant from the State to the grantee or grantees named and for the lands described therein. (1915, c. 249, s. 1; C.S., s. 1752; 1961, c. 740, s. 2; 1973, c. 476, s. 48.)

§ 8-8. Certified copies of grants and abstracts recorded.

Duly certified copies of such grants and of such memoranda and abstracts of grants may be recorded in the county where the lands therein described are situated, and the records thereof in such counties, or certified copies thereof, shall likewise be competent evidence for the purpose of showing title from the State of North Carolina to the grantee or grantees named and for the lands described therein. (1915, c. 249, s. 2; C.S., s. 1753.)

§ 8-9. Copies of grants certified by clerk of Secretary of State validated.

All copies of grants heretofore issued from the office of the Secretary of State, duly certified under the great seal of the State, and to which the name of the Secretary has been written or affixed by the clerk of the said Secretary of State, are hereby ratified and approved and declared to be good and valid copies of the original grants and admissible in evidence in all courts of this State when duly registered in the counties in which the land lies; all such copies heretofore registered in said counties are hereby declared to be lawful and regular in all respects as if the same had been signed by the Secretary of State in person and duly registered. (1901, c. 613; Rev., s. 1597; C.S., s. 1754.)

§ 8-10. Copies of grants in Burke.

Copies of grants issued by the State within the County of Burke prior to the destruction of the records of said county by General Stoneman in the year 1865, shall be admitted in evidence in all actions when the same are duly registered; and when the original grants are lost, destroyed or cannot be found after due search, it shall be presumed that the same were duly registered within the time prescribed by law, as provided upon the face of original grant. (1901, c. 513; Rev., s. 1610; C.S., s. 1755.)

§ 8-11. Copies of grants in Moore.

Copies of grants for land situated in Moore County and the counties of which Moore was a part, entered in a book, and the book being certified under the seal of the Secretary of State, shall have the force and effect of the originals and be evidence in all courts. (1903, c. 214; Rev., s. 1613; C.S., s. 1756.)

§ 8-12. Copies of grants in Onslow.

The copies of grants made by the register of deeds of Onslow County under laws of 1907, chapter 434, of grants, abstracts of grants, and other documents pertaining to titles of land in Onslow County issued prior to the year 1800, and contained in a book called Book of Transcribed Grants Issued Prior to One Thousand Eight Hundred, duly authenticated as prescribed in said Chapter 434 of the laws of 1907, shall be received as evidence in all courts of the State, and certified copies therefrom shall be received as evidence. (1907, c. 434; C.S., s. 1757.)

§ 8-13. Certain deeds dated before 1835 evidence of due execution.

In all actions hereafter instituted in which the title or ownership of any lands situated in North Carolina is at issue or in dispute, any deed or release, or a duly certified copy thereof, in which the people of the State of North Carolina are grantees and bearing date prior to the year 1835 and purporting to have been filed and recorded in the office of the Secretary of State of North Carolina prior to said year and now on file and of record in said office, and executed or purporting to have been executed by any person or persons as the representatives or agents or for or on behalf of any society, tribe, nation or aggregation of persons, whether signed or executed individually or in their representative capacity, and any such deed or release having been authorized to be executed by an act of the General Assembly of North Carolina by the properly authorized agents of such society, tribe, nation or aggregation of persons, shall be prima facie evidence that the person or persons signing or executing any such deed or release were the properly authorized agent or agents of such society, tribe, nation or aggregation of persons. Any recitals or statements of fact in any such deed or release shall be prima facie evidence of the truth thereof in any such actions. (1915, c. 75; C.S., s. 1758.)

§ 8-14. Certified copies of maps of Cherokee lands.

Certified copies by the Secretary of State of the copies, or parts thereof, of the maps of the Cherokee lands and of the Cherokee Country, as provided for and described in Chapter 175 of the laws of 1911, shall have the same force and effect and be entitled to the same force and effect as evidence as certified copies of the whole or parts of the original maps. (1911, c. 175; C.S., s. 1759.)

§ 8-15. Certified copies of certain surveys and maps obtained from the State of Tennessee.

A certified copy of the report of the survey made by the North Carolina commissioners, McDowell, Vance and Matthews, of that portion of the State of Tennessee extending from a point on the Virginia line to a point on the Smoky Mountain west of the Pigeon River, as obtained and filed by the Secretary of State under the provisions of Chapter 162 of the laws of 1913, shall, when certified under the hand and seal of the Secretary of State, be competent evidence in the trial of any action in the courts of the State. (1913, c. 162; C.S., s. 1760.)

§ 8-16. Evidence of title under H.E. McCulloch grants.

In all actions or suits, wherein it may be necessary for either party to prove title, by virtue of a grant or grants made by the king of Great Britain or Earl Granville to Henry McCulloch, or Henry Eustace McCulloch, it shall be sufficient for such party, in the usual manner, to give evidence of the grant or conveyance from the king of Great Britain or Earl Granville to the said Henry McCulloch, or Henry Eustace McCulloch, and the mesne conveyances thereafter, without giving any evidence of the deed or deeds of release, relinquishment or confirmation of Earl Granville to the said Henry McCulloch, or Henry Eustace McCulloch, or the power or powers of attorney by which the conveyances from the said Henry McCulloch, or Henry Eustace McCulloch, purport to have been made. (1819, c. 1021, P.R.; R.C., c. 44, s. 1; Code, s. 1336; Rev., s. 1600; C.S., s. 1761.)

§ 8-17. Conveyances or certified copies evidence of title under McCulloch.

In all trials where the title of either plaintiff or defendant shall be derived from Henry Eustace McCulloch, or Henry McCulloch, out of their tracts numbers one and three, it shall not be required of such party to produce, in support of his title, either the original grant from the crown to the proprietors, or a registered copy thereof; but in all such cases the grant or deed executed by such reputed proprietors, or by his or their lawful attorney, or a certified copy thereof, shall be deemed and held sufficient proof of the title of such proprietors, in the same manner as though the original grants were produced in evidence. (1807, c. 724, P.R.; R.C., c. 44, s. 2; Code, s. 1337; Rev., s. 1601; C.S., s. 1762.)

§ 8-18. Certified copies of registered instruments evidence.

A copy of the record of any deed, mortgage, power of attorney, or other instrument required or allowed to be registered, duly authenticated by the certificate and official seal of the register of deeds of the county where the original or duly certified copy has been registered, may be given in evidence in any of the courts of the State where the original of such copy would be admitted as evidence, although the party offering the same shall be entitled to the possession of the original, and shall not account for the nonproduction thereof, unless by a rule or order of the court, made upon affidavit suggesting some material variance from the original in such registry or other sufficient grounds, such party shall have been previously required to produce the original, in which case the same shall be produced or its absence duly accounted for according to the course and practice of the court. (1846, c. 68, s. 1; R.C., c. 37, s. 16; Code, s. 1251; 1893, c. 119, s. 2; Rev., s. 1598; C.S., s. 1763.)

§ 8-19. Common survey of contiguous tracts evidence.

Whenever any person owns several tracts of land which are contiguous or adjoining, but held under different deeds and different surveys, it may be lawful for any such person to have all such bodies of land included in one common survey by running around the lines of the outer tracts, and thereupon the possession of any part of said land covered by such common survey shall be deemed and held in law as a possession of the whole and every part thereof: Provided, that nothing in this section shall be construed to affect the rights or claims of persons which have already accrued to any part of said land. In all cases where such common surveys are made as directed by this section, the same may be recorded and registered as in cases of deeds, and shall be evidence in like manner. (1869-70, c. 34, ss. 1, 2; Code, s. 1277; Rev., s. 1505; C.S., s. 1764.)

§ 8-20: Repealed by Session Laws 1993, c. 288, s. 1.

§ 8-21. Deeds and records thereof lost, presumed to be in due form.

Whenever it is shown in any judicial proceeding that a deed or conveyance of real estate has been lost or destroyed, and that the same had been registered, and that the register's book containing the copy has been destroyed by fire or other accident, so that a copy thereof cannot be had, it shall be presumed and held, unless the contents be shown to have been otherwise, that such deed or conveyance transferred an estate in fee simple, if the grantor was entitled to such an estate at the time of conveyance, and that it was made upon sufficient consideration. (1854, c. 17; R.C., c. 44, s. 14; Code, s. 1348; Rev., s. 1602; C.S., s. 1766.)

§ 8-22. Local: recitals in tax deeds in Haywood and Henderson.

In all legal controversies touching lands in the Counties of Haywood and Henderson, in which either party shall claim title under any sale for taxes alleged to have been due and laid, in and for the year one thousand seven hundred and ninety-six, or any preceding year, the recital contained in the deed or assurance, made by the sheriff or other officer conveying or assuring the same, of the taxes having been laid and assessed, and of the same having remained due and unpaid, shall be held and taken to be prima facie evidence of the truth of each and every of the matters so recited. (R.C., c. 44, s. 11; Code, s. 1346; Rev., s. 1606, C.S., s. 1767.)

§ 8-22.1. Local: tax deeds in Richmond.

Proof of execution and delivery of a deed recorded before 1971 to a grantee by the sheriff of Richmond County pursuant to sale under execution in a tax foreclosure proceeding brought by Richmond County under G.S. 105-375 establishes a presumption that all notices required by G.S. 105-375 and Article 29B of Chapter 1 of the General Statutes were duly given and served, as required by law, to all persons entitled to receive the notices. (1981, c. 517.)

§ 8-23. Local: copies of records from Tyrrell.

Copies of records of the County of Tyrrell between the years one thousand seven hundred and thirty-five and one thousand seven hundred and ninety-nine, when copied in a book and certified to by the clerk of the Superior Court of Tyrrell County as to the records of his office and by the register of deeds as to the records of his office, and deposited in their respective offices in Washington County, shall be treated in all respects as original records and received as evidence in all courts of Washington County. (1903, c. 199; Rev., s. 1612, C.S., s. 1768.)

§ 8-24. Local: records of partition in Duplin.

The transcripts made by the clerk of the Superior Court of Duplin County, in accordance with Chapter three hundred and ninety-five of the laws of one thousand nine hundred and seven, of the reports of committees relating to the partition of real estate on file in his office prior and up to the year one thousand eight hundred and fifty-six, entered and indexed in a book entitled Reports of Committees, A, and the reports of committees beginning with and subsequent to the year one thousand eight hundred and fifty-six, entered and indexed in a book entitled Reports of Committees, B, shall be as competent evidence as are the original reports of the committees. (1907, c. 395, ss. 3, 4; C.S., s. 1769.)

§ 8-25. Local: records of wills in Duplin.

The transcripts made by the clerk of the Superior Court of Duplin County, in accordance with Chapter three hundred and ninety-five of the laws of one thousand nine hundred and seven, of all wills and entries of probate and dates of registration appearing on the same, on file in his office prior and up to the

January term of the County Court of Duplin County, one thousand eight hundred and thirty, and entered in a book designated as Records of Wills, A, and duly indexed as provided by law, shall be as competent evidence in any court as are the originals of such wills. (1907, c. 395, ss. 1, 2; C.S., s. 1770.)

§ 8-26. Local: records of deeds and wills in Anson.

The copies of the deeds and deed books and of the wills and will books made in Anson County under the act of March second, one thousand nine hundred and five, shall have the same force and effect as the original deeds and deed books copied and as the original wills and will books copied, and shall take the place of said original deeds and deed books and wills and will books as evidence in all court procedure; and wherever said deed books or will books are ordered or directed to be produced in court by subpoena or other order of court, the copies made under such act shall be produced, unless the court shall specially order the production of the original books, and the copies so produced in court shall have the same validity and effect and be used for the same purposes, with the same effect, as the original books. (1905, c. 663, s. 3; Rev., s. 1615; C.S., s. 1771.)

§ 8-27. Local: records of wills in Brunswick.

Under the provisions of Chapter one hundred and six of the laws of one thousand nine hundred and eight, authorizing and directing that all unrecorded wills, dated prior to January first, one thousand eight hundred and seventy-five, on file in the office of the clerk of the Superior Court of Brunswick County, and which have been duly proved in the form required by law, and bearing the adjudication certificate of the proper officer, shall be recorded in the books of wills in the said office and properly indexed; that all wills recorded in the minutes of the court of pleas and quarter sessions or other books of record in said office shall be transcribed and indexed in the book of wills in said office; and that all wills recorded in the office of the register of deeds of said county shall be properly indexed in the book kept for the purpose in the office of the clerk of the superior court of the county; the record of any instrument or certified copy thereof, recorded under the provisions of this Article, shall be admitted in evidence in the trial of any cause, subject to the same rules upon which other wills are admitted. (1908, s. 106; C.S., s. 1772.)

§ 8-28. Copies of wills.

Copies of wills, duly certified by the proper officer, may be given in evidence in any proceeding wherein the contents of the will may be competent evidence. (1784, c. 225, s. 6, P.R.; R.C., c. 119, s. 21; Code, s. 2175; Rev., s. 1603; C.S., s. 1773.)

§ 8-29. Copies of wills in Secretary of State's office.

Copies of wills filed or recorded in the office of the Secretary of State, attested by the Secretary, may be given in evidence in any court, and shall be taken as sufficient proof of the devise of real estate, and are declared good and effectual to pass the estate therein devised: Provided, that no such will may be given in evidence in any court nor taken as sufficient proof of the devise unless a certificate of probate appear thereon. (1852, c. 172; R.C., c. 44, s. 12; 1856-7, c. 22; Code, s. 2181; Rev., s. 1607; C.S., s. 1774.)

§ 8-30. Copies of wills recorded in wrong county.

Whereas, by reason of the uncertainty of the boundary lines of many of the counties of the State, wills have been proved, recorded and registered in the wrong county, whereby titles are insecure; for remedy whereof: The registry or duly certified copy of the record of any will, duly recorded, may be given in evidence in any of the courts of this State. (1858-9, c. 18; Code, s. 2182; Rev., s. 1608; C.S., s. 1775.)

§ 8-31. Copy of will proved and lost before recorded.

When any will which has been proved and ordered to be recorded was destroyed during the war between the states, before it was recorded, a copy of such will, so entitled to be admitted to record, though not certified by any officer, shall, when the court shall be satisfied of the genuineness thereof, be ordered to be recorded, and shall be received in evidence whenever the original or duly certified exemplification would be; and such copies may be proved and admitted to record under the same rules, regulations and restrictions as are prescribed in Chapter 98 entitled Burnt and Lost Records. (1866-7, c. 127; Code, s. 2183; Rev., s. 1609; C.S., s. 1776.)

§ 8-32. Certified copies of deeds and wills from other states.

In cases where inhabitants of other states or territories, by will or deed, devise or convey property situated in this State, and the original will or deed cannot be obtained for registration in the county where the land lies, or where the property shall be in dispute, a copy of said will or deed (after the same has been proved and registered or deposited, agreeable to the laws of the state where the person died or made the same) being properly certified, either according to the act of Congress or by the proper officer of the said state or territory, shall be read as evidence. (1802, c. 623, P.R.; R.C., c. 44, s. 9; Code, s. 1344; Rev., s. 1619; C.S., s. 1777.)

§ 8-33. Copies of lost records in Bladen.

The clerk of the Superior Court of Bladen County shall transcribe the judgment docket and index books and the will books in his office, and all other books in said office containing records made since the year one thousand eight hundred and sixty-eight, and the records so transcribed shall have the same force and effect as the original records would have, and shall be received in evidence as the original records and be prima facie evidence of their correctness and of the sufficiency of their probate, though the probates are lost and are not transcribed. (1895, c. 415; 1903, c. 65; Rev., s. 1611; C.S., s. 1778.)

Article 3.

Public Records.

§ 8-34. Copies of official writings.

(a) Copies of all official bonds, writings, papers, or documents, recorded or filed as records in any court, or public office, or lodged in the office of the Governor, Treasurer, Auditor, Secretary of State, Attorney General, Adjutant General, or the State Department of Cultural Resources, shall be as competent evidence as the originals, when certified by the keeper of such records or writings under the seal of the keeper's office when there is such seal, or under the keeper's hand when there is no such seal, unless the court shall order the production of the original. Copies of the records of the board of county commissioners shall be evidence when certified by the clerk of the board under the clerk's hand and seal of the county.

(b) The provisions of this section shall apply to records stored on any form of permanent, computer-readable media, such as a CD-ROM, if the medium is not subject to erasure or alteration. Nonerasable, computer-readable storage media may be used for preservation duplicates, as defined in G.S. 132-8.2, or for the preservation of permanently valuable records as provided in G.S. 121-5(d). (1792, c. 368, s. 11, P.R.; R.C., c. 44, s. 8; 1868-9, c. 20, s. 21; 1871-2, c. 91; Code, ss. 715, 1342; Rev., s. 1616; C.S., s. 1779; 1961, c. 739; 1973, c. 476, s. 48; 1999-131, s. 3; 1999-456, s. 47(c); 2011-326, s. 13(a).)

§ 8-35. Authenticated copies of public records.

All copies of bonds, contracts, notes, mortgages, or other papers relating to or connected with any loan, account, settlement of any account or any part thereof, or other transaction, between the United States or any state thereof or any corporation all of whose stock is beneficially owned by the United States or any state thereof, either directly or indirectly, and any person, natural or artificial; or extracts therefrom when complete on any one subject, or copies from the books or papers on file, or records of any public office of the State or the United States or of any corporation all of whose stock is beneficially owned by the United States or by any state thereof, directly or indirectly, shall be received in evidence and entitled to full faith and credit in any of the courts of this State when certified to by the chief officer or agent in charge of such public office or of such office of such corporation, or by the secretary or an assistant secretary of such corporation, to be true copies, and authenticated under the seal of the office, department, or corporation concerned. Any such certificate shall be prima facie evidence of the genuineness of such certificate and seal, the truth of the statements made in such certificate, and the official character of the person by which it purports to have been executed. (1891, c. 501; Rev., s. 1617; C.S., s. 1780; 1939, c. 149.)

§ 8-35.1. Division of Motor Vehicles' record admissible as prima facie evidence of convictions of offenses involving impaired driving.

Notwithstanding the provisions of G.S. 15A-924(d), a properly certified copy under G.S. 8-35 or G.S. 20-26(b) of the license records of a defendant kept by the Division of Motor Vehicles under G.S. 20-26(a) is admissible as prima facie evidence of any prior conviction of a defendant for an offense involving impaired driving as defined in G.S. 20-4.01(24a). (1975, c. 642, s. 1; c. 716, s. 5; 1983, c. 435, s. 3.)

§ 8-35.2. Records of clerk of court criminal index admissible in certain cases.

Notwithstanding the provisions of G.S. 15A-924(d) or 15A-1340.4(e), certified copies of the records contained in the criminal index or similar records maintained manually or by automatic data processing equipment by the clerk of superior court, are admissible as prima facie evidence of any prior convictions of the person named in the records, if the original documents upon which the records are based have been destroyed pursuant to law. The index must contain at least the following information:

(1)   The case file number;

(2)   The name, sex, and race of the defendant;

(3)   His address;

(4)   His driver's license number, if the conviction is for a motor vehicle offense and the number is available;

(5)   The date of birth of the defendant, if it is available;

(6)   The offense for which he was charged and the date of same;

(7)   The disposition of the charge and the date of same;

(8)   Whether the defendant was indigent;

(9)   Whether he was represented by an attorney, and if so, the name of the attorney;

(10)   Whether the defendant waived his right to an attorney, and

(11)   The name and address of any victim, if available. (1985, c. 606, s. 1; 1997-456, s. 27.)

§ 8-36. Authenticated copy of record of administration.

When letters testamentary or of administration on the goods and chattels of any person deceased, being an inhabitant in another state or territory, have been granted, or a return or inventory of the estate has been made, a copy of the record of administration or of the letters testamentary, and a copy of an inventory or return of the effects of the deceased, after the same has been granted or made, agreeable to the laws of the state where the same has been done, being properly certified, either according to the act of Congress or by the proper officer of such state or territory, shall be allowed as evidence. (1834, c. 4; R.C., c. 44, s. 7; Code, s. 1343; Rev., s. 1618; C.S., s. 1781.)

§ 8-37. Certificate of Commissioner of Motor Vehicles as to ownership of automobile.

In any civil or criminal action in which the ownership of a motor vehicle is relevant, evidence as to the letters and numbers appearing upon the registration plate attached to such vehicle or of the motor vehicle identification number, together with certified copies of records furnished pursuant to G.S. 20-42 by the Commissioner of Motor Vehicles showing the name of the owner of the vehicle to which such registration plate or vehicle identification number is assigned, or a certified copy of the certificate of title for such motor vehicle on file with the Commissioner of Motor Vehicles, is prima facie evidence of the ownership of such motor vehicle. (1931, c. 88, s. 1; 1943, c. 650; 1979, c. 980.)

Article 3A.

Findings, Records and Reports of Federal Officers and Employees.

§ 8-37.1. Finding of presumed death.

(a) A written finding of presumed death, made by the Secretary of War, the Secretary of the Navy, or other officer or employee of the United States authorized to make such finding, pursuant to the Federal Missing Persons Act (56 Stat. 143, 1092, and P.L. 408, ch. 371, 2d Sess. 78th Cong.; 50 U.S.C. App. Supp. 1001-17), as now or hereafter amended, or a duly certified copy of such finding, shall be received in any court, office or other place in this State as prima facie evidence of the death of the person therein found to be dead, and the date, circumstances and place of his disappearance. This subsection applies only to findings of presumed death made prior to the effective date of Section 5(b) of Public Law 89-554.

(b) A written finding of presumed death, made by the Secretary pursuant to Chapter 10 of Title 37 of the U.S. Code, P.L. 89-554 as now or hereafter amended, or a duly certified copy of such finding, shall be received in any court, office, or other place in this State as prima facie evidence of the death of the person therein found to be dead, and the date, circumstances, and place of his disappearance. This subsection applies only to findings of presumed death made on or after the effective date of Section 5(b) of Public Law 89-554. (1945, c. 731, s. 1; 1995, c. 379, s. 3.)

§ 8-37.2. Report or record that person missing, interned, captured, etc.

An official written report or record, or duly certified copy thereof, that a person is missing, missing in action, interned in a neutral country, or beleaguered, besieged or captured by an enemy, or is dead, or is alive, made by any officer or employee of the United States authorized by the act referred to in § 8-37.1, or by any other law of the United States to make same, shall be received in any court, office or other place in this State as prima facie evidence that such person is missing, missing in action, interned in a neutral country, or beleaguered, besieged or captured by an enemy, or is dead, or is alive, as the case may be. (1945, c. 731, s. 2.)

§ 8-37.3. Deemed signed and issued pursuant to law; evidence of authority to certify.

For the purposes of §§ 8-37.1 and 8-37.2 any finding, report or record, or duly certified copy thereof, purporting to have been signed by such an officer or employee of the United States as is described in said sections, shall prima facie be deemed to have been signed and issued by such an officer or employee pursuant to law, and the person signing same shall prima facie be deemed to have acted within the scope of his authority. If a copy purports to have been certified by a person authorized by law to certify the same, such certified copy shall be prima facie evidence of his authority so to certify. (1945, c. 731, s. 3.)

Article 4.

Other Writings in Evidence.

§ 8-38: Repealed by Session Laws 1983 (Regular Session, 1984), c. 1037, s. 13.

§ 8-39. Parol evidence to identify land described.

In all actions for the possession of or title to any real estate parol testimony may be introduced to identify the land sued for, and fit it to the description contained in the paper-writing offered as evidence of title or of the right of possession, and if from this evidence the jury is satisfied that the land in question is the identical land intended to be conveyed by the parties to such paper-writing, then such paper-writing shall be deemed and taken to be sufficient in law to pass such title to or interest in such land as it purports to pass: Provided, that such paper-writing is in all other respects sufficient to pass such title or interest. (1891, c. 465, s. 1; Rev., s. 1605; C.S., s. 1783.)

§ 8-40: Repealed by Session Laws 1983 (Regular Session, 1984), c. 1037, s. 12.

§ 8-40.1: Repealed by Session Laws 1983 (Regular Session, 1984), c. 1037, s. 10.

§ 8-41. Bills of lading in evidence.

In all actions by or against common carriers or in the trial of any criminal action in which it shall be thought necessary to introduce in evidence any bills of lading issued by said common carrier or by a connecting carrier, it shall be competent to introduce in evidence any paper-writing purporting to be the original bill of lading, or a duplicate thereof, upon proof that such paper purporting to be such bill of lading or duplicate was received in due course of mail from consignor or agent of said carrier or connecting carrier, or delivered by said common carrier to the consignee or other person entitled to the possession of the property for which said paper purports to be the bill of lading: Provided, that such purported bill of lading shall not be declared to be the bill of lading unless the said purported bill of lading is first exhibited by the plaintiff or his agent or attorney to the defendant or its attorney, or its agent upon whom process may be served, ten days before the trial where the point of shipment is in the State, and twenty days when the point of shipment is without the State. Upon such proof and introduction of the bill of lading, the due execution thereof shall be prima facie established. (1915, c. 287; C.S., s. 1785; 1945, c. 97.)

§ 8-42. Book accounts under sixty dollars.

When any person shall bring an action upon a contract, or shall plead, or give notice of, a setoff or counterclaim for goods, wares and merchandise by him sold and delivered, or for work done and performed, he shall file his account with his complaint, or with his plea or notice of setoff or counterclaim, and if upon the trial of the issue, or executing a writ of inquiry of damages in such action, he shall declare upon his oath that the matter in dispute is a book account, and that he hath no means to prove the delivery of any of the articles which he then shall propose to prove by himself but by this book, in that case such book may be given in evidence, if he shall make out by his own oath that it doth contain a true account of all the dealings, or the last settlement of accounts between himself and the opposing party, and that all the articles therein contained, and by him so proved, were bona fide delivered, and that he hath given the opposing party all just credits; and such book and oath shall be received as evidence for the several articles so proved to be delivered within two years next before the commencement of the action, but not for any article of a longer standing, nor for any greater amount than sixty dollars ($60.00). (1756, c. 57, ss. 2, 6, 7, P.R.; R.C., c. 15, s. 1; Code, s. 591; Rev., s. 1622; C.S., s. 1786.)

§ 8-43. Book accounts proved by personal representative.

In all actions where executors and administrators are parties, such book account for all articles delivered within two years previous to the death of the deceased may be proved under the like circumstances, rules and conditions; and in such case, the executor or administrator may prove by himself that he found the account so stated on the books of the deceased; that there are no witnesses, to his knowledge, capable of proving the delivery of the articles which he shall propose to prove by said book, and that he believes the same to be just, and doth not know of any other or further credit to be given than what is therein mentioned: Provided, that if two years shall not have elapsed previous to the death of the deceased, the executor or administrator may prove the said book account, if the suit shall be commenced within three years from the delivery of the articles: Provided further, that whenever by the aforesaid proviso the time of proving a book account in manner aforesaid is enlarged as to the one party, to the same extent shall be enlarged the time as to the other party. (1756, c. 57, s. 2, P.R.; 1796, c. 465, P.R.; R.C., c. 15, s. 2; Code, s. 592; Rev., s. 1623; C.S., s. 1787.)

§ 8-44. Copies of book accounts in evidence.

A copy from the book of accounts proved in manner above directed may be given in evidence in any such action or setoff as aforesaid, and shall be as available as if such book had been produced, unless the party opposing such proof shall give notice to the adverse party or his attorney, at the joining of the issue, or 10 days before the trial, that he will require the book to be produced at the trials; and in that case no such copy shall be admitted as evidence. (1756, c. 57, s. 33, P.R.; R.C., c. 15, s. 3; C.C.P., s. 343c; Code, s. 593; Rev., s. 1624; C.S., s. 1788.)

§ 8-44.1. Hospital medical records.

Copies or originals of hospital medical records shall not be held inadmissible in any court action or proceeding on the grounds that they lack certification, identification, or authentication, and shall be received as evidence if otherwise admissible, in any court or quasi-judicial proceeding, if they have been tendered to the presiding judge or designee by the custodian of the records, in accordance with G.S. 1A-1, Rule 45(c), or if they are certified, identified, and authenticated by the live testimony of the custodian of such records.

Hospital medical records are defined for purposes of this section and G.S. 1A-1, Rule 45(c) as records made in connection with the diagnosis, care and treatment of any patient or the charges for such services except that records covered by G.S. 122-8.1, G.S. 90-109.1 and federal statutory or regulatory provisions regarding alcohol and drug abuse, are subject to the requirements of said statutes. (1973, c. 1332, s. 1; 1983, c. 665, s. 2.)

§ 8-45. Itemized and verified accounts.

In any actions instituted in any court of this State upon an account for goods sold and delivered, for rents, for services rendered, or labor performed, or upon any oral contract for money loaned, a verified itemized statement of such account shall be received in evidence, and shall be deemed prima facie evidence of its correctness. (1897, c. 480; Rev., s. 1625; 1917, c. 32; C.S., s. 1789; 1941, c. 104.)

Article 4A.

Photographic Copies of Business and Public Records.

§ 8-45.1. Photographic reproductions admissible; destruction of originals.

(a)   If any business, institution, member of a profession or calling, or any department or agency of government, in the regular course of business or activity has kept or recorded any memorandum, writing, entry, print, representation, X ray or combination thereof, of any act, transaction, occurrence or event, and in the regular course of business has caused any or all of the same to be recorded, copied or reproduced by any photographic, photostatic, microfilm, microcard, miniature photographic, or other process which accurately reproduces or forms a durable medium for so reproducing the original, the original may be destroyed in the regular course of business unless held in a custodial or fiduciary capacity or unless its preservation is required by law. Such reproduction, when satisfactorily identified, is as admissible in evidence as the original itself in any judicial or administrative proceeding whether the original is in existence or not and an enlargement or facsimile of such reproduction is likewise admissible in evidence if the original reproduction is in existence and available for inspection under direction of court. The introduction of a reproduced record, enlargement or facsimile, does not preclude admission of the original.

(b)   The provisions of subsection (a) of this section shall apply to records stored on any form of permanent, computer-readable media, such as a CD-ROM, if the medium is not subject to erasure or alteration. Nonerasable, computer-readable storage media may be used for preservation duplicates, as defined in G.S. 132-8.2, or for the preservation of permanently valuable records as provided in G.S. 121-5(d). (1951, ch. 262, s. 1; 1977, ch. 569; 1999-131, s. 1; 1999-456, s. 47(a); 2011-326, s. 13(b).)

§ 8-45.2. Uniformity of interpretation.

This Article shall be so interpreted and construed as to effectuate its general purpose of making uniform the law of those states which enact it. (1951, c. 262, s. 2.)

§ 8-45.3. Photographic reproduction of records of Department of Revenue and Division of Employment Security.

(a) The State Department of Revenue is hereby specifically authorized to have photographed, photocopied, or microphotocopied all records of the Department, including tax returns required by law to be made to the Department, and said photographs, photocopies, or microphotocopies, when certified by the Department as true and correct photographs, photocopies, or microphotocopies, shall be as admissible in evidence in all actions, proceedings and matters as the originals thereof would have been.

(a1) The Division of Employment Security is hereby specifically authorized to have photographed, photocopied, or microphotocopied all records of the Division, including filings required by law to be made to the Division, and said photographs, photocopies, or microphotocopies, when certified by the Division as true and correct photographs, photocopies, or microphotocopies, shall be as admissible in evidence in all actions, proceedings, and matters as the originals thereof would have been.

(b) The provisions of this section shall apply to records stored on any form of permanent, computer-readable media, such as a CD-ROM, if the medium is not subject to erasure or alteration. Nonerasable, computer-readable storage media may be used for preservation duplicates, as defined in G.S. 132-8.2, or for the preservation of permanently valuable records as provided in G.S. 121-5(d). (1951, c. 262, s. 3; 1999-131, s. 2; 1999-456, s. 47(b); 2001-115, s. 1; 2011-326, s. 13(c); 2011-401, s. 3.2.)

§ 8-45.4. Title of Article.

This Article may be cited as the "Uniform Photographic Copies of Business and Public Records as Evidence Act." (1951, c. 262, s. 4.)

Article 4B.

Evidence of Fraud, Duress, Undue Influence.

§ 8-45.5. Statements, releases, etc., obtained from persons in shock or under the influence of drugs; fraud presumed.

Any oral or written statement, waiver, release, receipt, or other representation of any kind by any person made or executed while a patient in any hospital and taken by any person in connection with any type of insurance coverage on or for the benefit of said patient which shall have been taken while such patient was in shock or appreciably under the influence of any drug, including drugs given primarily for sedation, shall be deemed to have been obtained by means of fraud, duress or undue influence on the part of the person or persons taking same, and the same shall be incompetent and inadmissible in evidence to prove or disprove any fact or circumstance relating to any claim for which any insurance company may be liable under any policy of insurance issued to, or which may indemnify or provide coverage or protection for the person making or executing any such statement or other instrument while a patient in a hospital, nor may any such person making or executing the same be examined or cross-examined in regard thereto. (1967, c. 928.)

Article 5.

Life Tables.

§ 8-46. Mortality tables as evidence.

Whenever it is necessary to establish the expectancy of continued life of any person from any period of the person's life, whether the person is living at the time or not, the table hereto appended shall be received in all courts and by all persons having power to determine litigation, as evidence, with other evidence as to the health, constitution and habits of the person, of such expectancy represented by the figures in the columns headed by the words "completed age" and "expectation" respectively:

Completed Age	Expectation
0	75.8
1	75.4
2	74.5
3	73.5
4	72.5

5	71.6
6	70.6
7	69.6
8	68.6
9	67.6
10	66.6
11	65.6
12	64.6
13	63.7
14	62.7
15	61.7
16	60.7
17	59.8
18	58.8
19	57.9
20	56.9
21	56.0
22	55.1
23	54.1
24	53.2
25	52.2

26	51.3
27	50.4
28	49.4
29	48.5
30	47.5
31	46.6
32	45.7
33	44.7
34	43.8
35	42.9
36	42.0
37	41.0
38	40.1
39	39.2
40	38.3
41	37.4
42	36.5
43	35.6
44	34.7
45	33.8
46	32.9

47	32.0
48	31.1
49	30.2
50	29.3
51	28.5
52	27.6
53	26.8
54	25.9
55	25.1
56	24.3
57	23.5
58	22.7
59	21.9
60	21.1
61	20.4
62	19.7
63	18.9
64	18.2
65	17.5
66	16.8
67	16.1

Age	Value
68	15.5
69	14.8
70	14.2
71	13.5
72	12.9
73	12.3
74	11.7
75	11.2
76	10.6
77	10.0
78	9.5
79	9.0
80	8.5
81	8.0
82	7.5
83	7.1
84	6.6
85 and over	6.6

(1883, c. 225; Code, s. 1352; Rev., s. 1626; C.S., s. 1790; 1955, c. 870; 1971, c. 968; 1997-133, s. 1.)

§ 8-47. Present worth of annuities.

Whenever it is necessary to establish the present worth or cash value of an annuity to a person, payable annually during the person's life, such present worth or cash value may be ascertained by the use of the following table in connection with the mortality tables established by law, the first column representing the number of years the annuity is to run and the second column representing the present cash value of an annuity of one dollar for such number of years, respectively:

No. of Years Annuity is to Run	Cash Value of the Annuity of $1
1	$ 0.943
2	1.833
3	2.673
4	3.465
5	4.212
6	4.917
7	5.582
8	6.210
9	6.802
10	7.360
11	7.887
12	8.384
13	8.853
14	9.295

15	....	9.712
16	....	10.106
17	....	10.477
18	....	10.828
19	....	11.158
20	....	11.470
21	....	11.764
22	....	12.042
23	....	12.303
24	....	12.550
25	....	12.783
26	....	13.003
27	....	13.211
28	....	13.406
29	....	13.591
30	....	13.765
31	....	13.929
32	....	14.084
33	....	14.230
34	....	14.368
35	....	14.498

36	....	14.621
37	....	14.737
38	....	14.846
39	....	14.949
40	....	15.046
41	....	15.138
42	....	15.225
43	....	15.306
44	....	15.383
45	....	15.456
46	....	15.524
47	....	15.589
48	....	15.650
49	....	15.708
50	....	15.762
51	....	15.813
52	....	15.861
53	....	15.907
54	....	15.950
55	....	15.991
56	....	16.029

Age	Value
57	16.065
58	16.099
59	16.131
60	16.161
61	16.190
62	16.217
63	16.242
64	16.266
65	16.289
66	16.310
67	16.331

The present cash value of the annuity for a fraction of a year may be ascertained as follows: Multiply the difference between the cash value of the annuities for the preceding and succeeding full years by the fraction of the year in decimals and add the sum to the present cash value for the preceding full year. When a person is entitled to the use of a sum of money for life, or for a given time, the interest thereon for one year, computed at four and one half percent (4 1/2%), may be considered as an annuity and the present cash value be ascertained as herein provided: Provided, the interest rate in computing the present cash value of a life interest in land shall be six percent (6%).

Whenever the mortality tables set out in G.S. 8-46 are admissible in evidence in any action or proceeding to establish the expectancy of continued life of any person from any period of the person's life, whether the person is living at the time or not, the annuity tables herein set forth shall be evidence, but not conclusive, of the loss of income during the period of life expectancy of the person. (1905, c. 347; Rev., s. 1627; C.S., s. 1791; 1927, c. 215; 1943, c. 543; 1957, c. 497; 1959, c. 879, s. 3; 1965, c. 991; 1997-133, s. 2.)

Article 6.

Calendars.

§ 8-48. Clark's Calendar; proof of dates.

(a) In any controversy or inquiry in any court or before any fact finding board, commission, administrative agency or other body, where it becomes necessary or pertinent to determine any information which may be established by reference to a calendar for any year between the years 1753 A.D. and 2002 A.D., inclusive, it is permissible to introduce in evidence "Clark's Calendar, a Calendar Covering 250 Years, 1753 A.D. to 2002 A.D.," as supplemented, copyrighted, 1940, by E. B. Clark, Entry: Class AA, Number 328,573, Copyright Office of the United States of America, Washington, or any reprint of the 1940 edition certified by the Secretary of State to be an accurate copy of it, and the calendar or reprint, when so introduced, shall be prima facie evidence that the information disclosed by the calendar or reprint is true and correct.

(b) The Secretary of State shall prepare and publish a perpetual calendar similar to Clark's Calendar covering years beginning with 2003 A.D. The perpetual calendar published by the Secretary of State shall be admissible in evidence to the same degree and in the same manner as Clark's Calendar for years beginning with 2003. (1941, c. 312; 1997-58, s. 1.)

Article 7.

Competency of Witnesses.

§ 8-49. Witness not excluded by interest or crime.

No person offered as a witness shall be excluded, by reason of incapacity from interest or crime, from giving evidence either in person or by deposition, according to the practice of the court, on the trial of any issue joined, or of any matter or question, or on any inquiry arising in any suit or proceeding, civil or criminal, in any court, or before any judge, justice, jury or other person having, by law, authority to hear, receive and examine evidence; and every person so offered shall be admitted to give evidence, notwithstanding such person may or shall have an interest in the matter in question, or in the event of the trial of the issue, or of the suit or other proceeding in which he is offered as a witness. This section shall not be construed to apply to attesting witnesses to wills. (1866, c. 43, ss. 1, 4; C.C.P., c. 342; 1869-70, c. 177; 1871-2, c. 4; Code, ss. 589, 1350; Rev., ss. 1628, 1629; C.S., s. 1792.)

§ 8-50. Parties competent as witnesses.

(a)   On the trial of any issue, or of any matter or question, or on any inquiry arising in any action, suit or other proceeding in court, or before any judge, justice, jury or other person having, by law, authority to hear and examine evidence, the parties themselves and the person in whose behalf any suit or other proceeding may be brought or defended, shall, except as otherwise provided, be competent and compellable to give evidence, either viva voce or by deposition, according to the practice of the court, in behalf of either or any of the parties to said action, suit or other proceeding. Nothing in this section shall be construed to apply to any action or other proceeding in any court instituted in consequence of adultery, or to any action for criminal conversation.

(b), (c). Repealed by Session Laws 1967, c. 954, s. 4. (1866, c. 43, ss. 2, 3; Code, s. 1351; Rev., s. 1630; C.S., s. 1793; 1953, c. 885, s. 1; 1967, c. 954, s. 4.)

§ 8-50.1. Competency of blood tests; jury charge; taxing of expenses as costs.

(a)   In the trial of any criminal action or proceeding in any court in which the question of parentage arises, regardless of any presumptions with respect to parentage, the court before whom the matter may be brought, upon motion of the State or the defendant, shall order that the alleged-parent defendant, the known natural parent, and the child submit to any blood tests and comparisons which have been developed and adapted for purposes of establishing or disproving parentage and which are reasonably accessible to the alleged-parent defendant, the known natural parent, and the child. The results of those blood tests and comparisons, including the statistical likelihood of the alleged parent's parentage, if available, shall be admitted in evidence when offered by a duly qualified, licensed practicing physician, duly qualified immunologist, duly qualified geneticist, or other duly qualified person. Upon receipt of a motion and the entry of an order under the provisions of this subsection, the court shall proceed as follows:

(1)   Where the issue of parentage is to be decided by a jury, where the results of those blood tests and comparisons are not shown to be inconsistent with the results of any other blood tests and comparisons, and where the results of those blood tests and comparisons indicate that the alleged-parent defendant cannot be the natural parent of the child, the jury shall be instructed that if they

believe that the witness presenting the results testified truthfully as to those results, and if they believe that the tests and comparisons were conducted properly, then it will be their duty to decide that the alleged-parent is not the natural parent; whereupon, the court shall enter the special verdict of not guilty; and

(2) By requiring the State or defendant, as the case may be, requesting the blood tests and comparisons pursuant to this subsection to initially be responsible for any of the expenses thereof and upon the entry of a special verdict incorporating a finding of parentage or nonparentage, by taxing the expenses for blood tests and comparisons, in addition to any fees for expert witnesses allowed per G.S. 7A-314 whose testimonies supported the admissibility thereof, as costs in accordance with G.S. 7A-304; G.S. Chapter 6, Article 7; or G.S. 7A-315, as applicable.

(b) Repealed by Session Laws 1993, c. 333, s. 2.

(b1) In the trial of any civil action in which the question of parentage arises, the court shall, on motion of a party, order the mother, the child, and the alleged father-defendant to submit to one or more blood or genetic marker tests, to be performed by a duly certified physician or other expert. The court shall require the person requesting the blood or genetic marker tests to pay the costs of the tests. The court may, in its discretion, tax as part of costs the expenses for blood or genetic marker tests and comparisons. Verified documentary evidence of the chain of custody of the blood specimens obtained pursuant to this subsection shall be competent evidence to establish the chain of custody. Any party objecting to or contesting the procedures or results of the blood or genetic marker tests shall file with the court written objections setting forth the basis for the objections and shall serve copies thereof upon all other parties not less than 10 days prior to any hearing at which the results may be introduced into evidence. The person contesting the results of the blood or genetic marker tests has the right to subpoena the testing expert pursuant to the Rules of Civil Procedure. If no objections are filed within the time and manner prescribed, the test results are admissible as evidence of paternity without the need for foundation testimony or other proof of authenticity or accuracy. The results of the blood or genetic marker tests shall have the following effect:

(1) If the court finds that the conclusion of all the experts, as disclosed by the evidence based upon the test, is that the probability of the alleged parent's parentage is less than eighty-five percent (85%), the alleged parent is presumed

not to be the parent and the evidence shall be admitted. This presumption may be rebutted only by clear, cogent, and convincing evidence;

(2)   If the experts disagree in their findings or conclusions, the question of paternity shall be submitted upon all the evidence;

(3)   If the tests show that the alleged parent is not excluded and that the probability of the alleged parent's parentage is between eighty-five percent (85%) and ninety-seven percent (97%), this evidence shall be admitted by the court and shall be weighed with other competent evidence;

(4)   If the experts conclude that the genetic tests show that the alleged parent is not excluded and that the probability of the alleged parent's parentage is ninety-seven percent (97%) or higher, the alleged parent is presumed to be the parent and this evidence shall be admitted. This presumption may be rebutted only by clear, cogent, and convincing evidence. (1949, c. 51; 1965, c. 618; 1975, c. 449, ss. 1, 2; 1979, c. 576, s. 1; 1993, c. 333, s. 2; 1993 (Reg. Sess., 1994), c. 733, s. 1.)

§ 8-50.2. Results of speed-measuring instruments; admissibility.

(a)   The results of the use of radio microwave, laser, or other speed-measuring instruments shall be admissible as evidence of the speed of an object in any criminal or civil proceeding for the purpose of corroborating the opinion of a person as to the speed of an object based upon the visual observation of the object by such person.

(b)   Notwithstanding the provisions of subsection (a) of this section, the results of a radio microwave, laser, or other electronic speed-measuring instrument are not admissible in any proceeding unless it is found that:

(1)   The operator of the instrument held, at the time the results of the speed-measuring instrument were obtained, a certificate from the North Carolina Criminal Justice Education and Training Standards Commission (hereinafter referred to as the Commission) authorizing him to operate the speed-measuring instrument from which the results were obtained.

(2)   The operator of the instrument operated the speed-measuring instrument in accordance with the procedures established by the Commission for the operation of such instrument.

(3) The instrument employed was approved for use by the Commission and the Secretary of Public Safety pursuant to G.S. 17C-6.

(4) The speed-measuring instrument had been calibrated and tested for accuracy in accordance with the standards established by the Commission for that particular instrument.

(c) All radio microwave, laser, and other electronic speed-measuring instruments shall be tested for accuracy within a 12-month period prior to the alleged violation by a technician possessing at least a General Radiotelephone Operator License from the Federal Communications Commissions or possessing a Certified Electronics Technician certificate issued by a Federal Communications Commission Commercial Operators License Examination Manager or by a laboratory established by the International Association of Chiefs of Police. A written certificate by the technician or laboratory showing that the test was made within the required period and that the instrument was accurate shall be competent and prima facie evidence of those facts in any proceeding referred to in subsection (a) of this section.

All radio microwave, laser, and other speed enforcement instruments shall be tested in accordance with standards established by the North Carolina Criminal Justice Education and Training Standards Commission. The Commission shall provide for certification of all radio microwave, laser, and other speed enforcement instruments.

(d) In every proceeding where the results of a radio microwave, laser, or other speed-measuring instrument is sought to be admitted, judicial notice shall be taken of the rules approving the use of the models and types of radio microwave, laser, and other speed-measuring instruments and the procedures for operation and calibration or measuring accuracy of such instruments. (1979, 2nd Sess., c. 1184, s. 3; 1983, c. 34; 1987, c. 318; c. 827, s. 60; 1994, Ex. Sess., c. 18, s. 1; 2005-137, s. 1; 2011-145, s. 19.1(g).)

§ 8-50.3: Expired September 30, 2007.

§ 8-51: Repealed by Session Laws 1983 (Regular Session, 1984), c. 1037, s. 5.

§ 8-51.1. Dying declarations.

Dying declarations admissible in administrative proceedings shall be as provided in G.S. 8C-1, Rule 804. (1973, c. 464, s. 1; 1983 (Reg. Sess., 1984), c. 1037, s. 11.)

§ 8-52. Repealed by Session Laws 1973, c. 41.

§ 8-53. Communications between physician and patient.

No person, duly authorized to practice physic or surgery, shall be required to disclose any information which he may have acquired in attending a patient in a professional character, and which information was necessary to enable him to prescribe for such patient as a physician, or to do any act for him as a surgeon, and no such information shall be considered public records under G.S. 132-1. Confidential information obtained in medical records shall be furnished only on the authorization of the patient, or if deceased, the executor, administrator, or, in the case of unadministered estates, the next of kin. Any resident or presiding judge in the district, either at the trial or prior thereto, or the Industrial Commission pursuant to law may, subject to G.S. 8-53.6, compel disclosure if in his opinion disclosure is necessary to a proper administration of justice. If the case is in district court the judge shall be a district court judge, and if the case is in superior court the judge shall be a superior court judge. (1885, c. 159; Rev., s. 1621; C.S., s. 1798; 1969, c. 914; 1977, c. 1118; 1983, c. 410, ss. 1, 2; c. 471.)

§ 8-53.1. Physician-patient and nurse privilege; limitations.

(a) Notwithstanding the provisions of G.S. 8-53 and G.S. 8-53.13, the physician-patient or nurse privilege shall not be a ground for excluding evidence regarding the abuse or neglect of a child under the age of 16 years or regarding an illness of or injuries to such child or the cause thereof in any judicial proceeding related to a report pursuant to the North Carolina Juvenile Code, Chapter 7B of the General Statutes of North Carolina.

(b) Nothing in this Article shall preclude a health care provider, as defined in G.S. 90-21.11, from disclosing information pursuant to G.S. 90-21.20B. (1965, c. 472, s. 2; 1971, c. 710, s. 2; 1981, c. 469, s. 24; 1998-202, s. 13(b); 2004-186, s. 16.2; 2006-253, s. 18; 2007-115, s. 4.)

§ 8-53.2. Communications between clergymen and communicants.

No priest, rabbi, accredited Christian Science practitioner, or a clergyman or ordained minister of an established church shall be competent to testify in any action, suit or proceeding concerning any information which was communicated to him and entrusted to him in his professional capacity, and necessary to enable him to discharge the functions of his office according to the usual course of his practice or discipline, wherein such person so communicating such information about himself or another is seeking spiritual counsel and advice relative to and growing out of the information so imparted, provided, however, that this section shall not apply where communicant in open court waives the privilege conferred. (1959, c. 646; 1963, c. 200; 1967, c. 794.)

§ 8-53.3. Communications between psychologist and client or patient.

No person, duly authorized as a licensed psychologist or licensed psychological associate, nor any of his or her employees or associates, shall be required to disclose any information which he or she may have acquired in the practice of psychology and which information was necessary to enable him or her to practice psychology. Any resident or presiding judge in the district in which the action is pending may, subject to G.S. 8-53.6, compel disclosure, either at the trial or prior thereto, if in his or her opinion disclosure is necessary to a proper administration of justice. If the case is in district court the judge shall be a district court judge, and if the case is in superior court the judge shall be a superior court judge.

Notwithstanding the provisions of this section, the psychologist-client or patient privilege shall not be grounds for failure to report suspected child abuse or neglect to the appropriate county department of social services, or for failure to report a disabled adult suspected to be in need of protective services to the appropriate county department of social services. Notwithstanding the provisions of this section, the psychologist-client or patient privilege shall not be grounds for excluding evidence regarding the abuse or neglect of a child, or an illness of or injuries to a child, or the cause thereof, or for excluding evidence regarding the abuse, neglect, or exploitation of a disabled adult, or an illness of or injuries to a disabled adult, or the cause thereof, in any judicial proceeding related to a report pursuant to the Child Abuse Reporting Law, Article 3 of Chapter 7B of the General Statutes, or to the Protection of the Abused, Neglected, or Exploited Disabled Adult Act, Article 6 of Chapter 108A of the General Statutes. (1967, c. 910, s. 18; 1983, c. 410, ss. 3, 7; 1987, c. 323, s. 2; 1993, c. 375, s. 2; c. 553, s. 78; 1998-202, s. 13(c).)

§ 8-53.4. School counselor privilege.

No person certified by the State Department of Public Instruction as a school counselor and duly appointed or designated as such by the governing body of a public school system within this State or by the head of any private school within this State shall be competent to testify in any action, suit, or proceeding concerning any information acquired in rendering counseling services to any student enrolled in such public school system or private school, and which information was necessary to enable him to render counseling services; provided, however, that this section shall not apply where the student in open court waives the privilege conferred. Any resident or presiding judge in the district in which the action is pending may compel disclosure, either at the trial or prior thereto, if in his opinion disclosure is necessary to a proper administration of justice. If the case is in district court the judge shall be the district court judge, and if the case is in superior court the judge shall be a superior court judge. (1971, c. 943; 1983, c. 410, ss. 4, 5.)

§ 8-53.5. Communications between licensed marital and family therapist and client(s).

No person, duly licensed as a licensed marriage and family therapist, nor any of the person's employees or associates, shall be required to disclose any information which the person may have acquired in rendering professional marriage and family therapy services, and which information was necessary to enable the person to render professional marriage and family therapy services. Any resident or presiding judge in the district in which the action is pending may, subject to G.S. 8-53.6, compel disclosure, either at the trial or prior thereto, if in the court's opinion disclosure is necessary to a proper administration of justice. If the case is in district court the judge shall be a district court judge, and if the case is in superior court the judge shall be a superior court judge. (1979, c. 697, s. 2; 1983, c. 410, ss. 6, 7; 1985, c. 223. s. 1; 2001-487, s. 40(a); 2004-203, s. 18.)

§ 8-53.6. No disclosure in alimony and divorce actions.

In an action pursuant to G.S. 50-5.1, 50-6, 50-7, 50-16.2A, and 50-16.3A if either or both of the parties have sought and obtained marital counseling by a licensed physician, licensed psychologist, licensed psychological associate, licensed clinical social worker, or licensed marriage and family therapist, the person or persons rendering such counseling shall not be competent to testify in the action concerning information acquired while rendering such counseling. (1983, c. 410, s. 8; 2001-152, s. 1.)

§ 8-53.7. Social worker privilege.

No person engaged in delivery of private social work services, duly licensed or certified pursuant to Chapter 90B of the General Statutes shall be required to disclose any information that he or she may have acquired in rendering professional social services, and which information was necessary to enable him or her to render professional social services: provided, that the presiding judge of a superior or district court may compel such disclosure, if in the court's opinion the same is necessary to a proper administration of justice and such disclosure is not prohibited by G.S. 8-53.6 or any other statute or regulation. (1983, c. 495, s. 2; 2001-152, s. 2; 2001-487, s. 40(b).)

§ 8-53.8. Counselor privilege.

No person, duly licensed pursuant to Chapter 90, Article 24, of the General Statutes, shall be required to disclose any information which he or she may have acquired in rendering professional counseling services, and which information was necessary to enable him or her to render professional counseling services: Provided, that the presiding judge of a superior or district court may compel such disclosure, if in the court's opinion the same is necessary to a proper administration of justice and such disclosure is not prohibited by other statute or regulation. (1983, c. 755, s. 2; 1993, c. 514, s. 2.)

§ 8-53.9. Optometrist/patient privilege.

No person licensed pursuant to Article 6 of Chapter 90 of the General Statutes shall be required to disclose any information that may have been acquired in rendering professional optometric services and which information was necessary to enable that person to render professional optometric services, except that the presiding judge of a superior or district court may compel this disclosure, if, in the court's opinion, disclosure is necessary to a proper administration of justice and disclosure is not prohibited by other statute or rule. (1997-75, s. 4; 1997-304, 3.)

§ 8-53.10. Peer support group counselors.

(a) Definitions. - The following definitions apply in this section:

(1) Client law enforcement employee. - Any law enforcement employee or a member of his or her immediate family who is in need of and receives peer counseling services offered by the officer's employing law enforcement agency.

(2) Immediate family. - A spouse, child, stepchild, parent, or stepparent.

(3) Peer counselor. - Any law enforcement officer or civilian employee of a law enforcement agency who:

a. Has received training to provide emotional and moral support and counseling to client law enforcement employees and their immediate families; and

b. Was designated by the sheriff, police chief, or other head of a law enforcement agency to counsel a client law enforcement employee.

(4) Privileged communication. - Any communication made by a client law enforcement employee or a member of the client law enforcement employee's immediate family to a peer counselor while receiving counseling.

(b) A peer counselor shall not disclose any privileged communication that was necessary to enable the counselor to render counseling services unless one of the following apply:

(1) The disclosure is authorized by the client or, if the client is deceased, the disclosure is authorized by the client's executor, administrator, or in the case of unadministrated estates, the client's next of kin.

(2) The disclosure is necessary to the proper administration of justice and, subject to G.S. 8-53.6, is compelled by a resident or presiding judge. If the case is in district court the judge shall be a district court judge, and if the case is in superior court the judge shall be a superior court judge.

(c) The privilege established by this section shall not apply:

(1) If the peer counselor was an initial responding officer, a witness, or a party to the incident that prompted the delivery of peer counseling services.

(2) To communications made while the peer counselor was not acting in his or her official capacity as a peer counselor.

(3) To communications related to a violation of criminal law. This subdivision does not require the disclosure of otherwise privileged communications related to an officer's use of force.

(d) Notwithstanding the provisions of this section, the peer counselor privilege shall not be grounds for failure to report suspected child abuse or neglect to the appropriate county department of social services, or for failure to report a disabled adult suspected to be in need of protective services to the appropriate county department of social services. Notwithstanding the provisions of this section, the peer counselor privilege shall not be grounds for excluding evidence regarding the abuse or neglect of a child, or an illness of or injuries to a child, or the cause thereof, or for excluding evidence regarding the abuse, neglect, or exploitation of a disabled adult, or an illness of or injuries to a disabled adult, or the cause thereof, in any judicial proceeding related to a report pursuant to the Child Abuse Reporting Law, Article 3 of Chapter 7B, or to the Protection of the Abused, Neglected, or Exploited Disabled Adult Act, Article 6 of Chapter 108A of the General Statutes. (1999-374, s. 1.)

§ 8-53.11. Persons, companies, or other entities engaged in gathering or dissemination of news.

(a) Definitions. - The following definitions apply in this section:

(1) Journalist. - Any person, company, or entity, or the employees, independent contractors, or agents of that person, company, or entity, engaged in the business of gathering, compiling, writing, editing, photographing, recording, or processing information for dissemination via any news medium.

(2) Legal proceeding. - Any grand jury proceeding or grand jury investigation; any criminal prosecution, civil suit, or related proceeding in any court; and any judicial or quasi-judicial proceeding before any administrative, legislative, or regulatory board, agency, or tribunal.

(3) News medium. - Any entity regularly engaged in the business of publication or distribution of news via print, broadcast, or other electronic means accessible to the general public.

(b)   A journalist has a qualified privilege against disclosure in any legal proceeding of any confidential or nonconfidential information, document, or item obtained or prepared while acting as a journalist.

(c)   In order to overcome the qualified privilege provided by subsection (b) of this section, any person seeking to compel a journalist to testify or produce information must establish by the greater weight of the evidence that the testimony or production sought:

(1)   Is relevant and material to the proper administration of the legal proceeding for which the testimony or production is sought;

(2)   Cannot be obtained from alternate sources; and

(3)   Is essential to the maintenance of a claim or defense of the person on whose behalf the testimony or production is sought.

Any order to compel any testimony or production as to which the qualified privilege has been asserted shall be issued only after notice to the journalist and a hearing and shall include clear and specific findings as to the showing made by the person seeking the testimony or production.

(d)   Notwithstanding subsections (b) and (c) of this section, a journalist has no privilege against disclosure of any information, document, or item obtained as the result of the journalist's eyewitness observations of criminal or tortious conduct, including any physical evidence or visual or audio recording of the observed conduct. (1999-267, s. 1.)

§ 8-53.12. Communications with agents of rape crisis centers and domestic violence programs privileged.

(a)   Definitions. - The following definitions apply in this section:

(1)   Agent. - An employee or agent of a center who has completed a minimum of 20 hours of training as required by the center, or a volunteer, under the direct supervision of a center supervisor, who has completed a minimum of 20 hours of training as required by the center.

(2)   Center. - A domestic violence program or rape crisis center.

(3) Domestic violence program. - A nonprofit organization or program whose primary purpose is to provide services to domestic violence victims.

(4) Domestic violence victim. - Any person alleging domestic violence as defined by G.S. 50B-1, who consults an agent of a domestic violence program for the purpose of obtaining, for himself or herself, advice, counseling, or other services concerning mental, emotional, or physical injuries suffered as a result of the domestic violence. The term shall also include those persons who have a significant relationship with a victim of domestic violence and who have sought, for themselves, advice, counseling, or other services concerning a mental, physical, or emotional condition caused or reasonably believed to be caused by the domestic violence against the victim.

(5) Rape crisis center. - Any publicly or privately funded agency, institution, organization, or facility that offers counseling and other services to victims of sexual assault and their families.

(6) Services. - Includes, but is not limited to, crisis hotlines; safe homes and shelters; assessment and intake; children of violence services; individual counseling; support in medical, administrative, and judicial systems; transportation, relocation, and crisis intervention. The term does not include investigation of physical or sexual assault of children under the age of 16.

(7) Sexual assault. - Any alleged violation of G.S. 14-27.2, 14-27.3, 14-27.4, 14-27.5, 14-27.7, 14-27.7A, or 14-202.1, whether or not a civil or criminal action arises as a result of the alleged violation.

(8) Sexual assault victim. - Any person alleging sexual assault, who consults an agent of a rape crisis center for the purpose of obtaining, for themselves, advice, counseling, or other services concerning mental, physical, or emotional injuries suffered as a result of sexual assault. The term shall also include those persons who have a significant relationship with a victim of sexual assault and who have sought, for themselves, advice, counseling, or other services concerning a mental, physical, or emotional condition caused or reasonably believed to be caused by sexual assault of a victim.

(9) Victim. - A sexual assault victim or a domestic violence victim.

(b) Privileged Communications. - No agent of a center shall be required to disclose any information which the agent acquired during the provision of services to a victim and which information was necessary to enable the agent to render the services; provided, however, that this subsection shall not apply where the victim waives the privilege conferred. Any resident or presiding judge in the district in which the action is pending shall compel disclosure, either at the trial or prior thereto, if the court finds, by a preponderance of the evidence, a good faith, specific and reasonable basis for believing that (i) the records or testimony sought contain information that is relevant and material to factual issues to be determined in a civil proceeding, or is relevant, material, and exculpatory upon the issue of guilt, degree of guilt, or sentencing in a criminal proceeding for the offense charged or any lesser included offense, (ii) the evidence is not sought merely for character impeachment purposes, and (iii) the evidence sought is not merely cumulative of other evidence or information available or already obtained by the party seeking the disclosure or the party's counsel. If the case is in district court, the judge shall be a district court judge, and if the case is in superior court, the judge shall be a superior court judge.

Before requiring production of records, the court must find that the party seeking disclosure has made a sufficient showing that the records are likely to contain information subject to disclosure under this subsection. If the court finds a sufficient showing has been made, the court shall order that the records be produced for the court under seal, shall examine the records in camera, and may allow disclosure of those portions of the records which the court finds contain information subject to disclosure under this subsection. After all appeals in the action have been exhausted, any records received by the court under seal shall be returned to the center, unless otherwise ordered by the court. The privilege afforded under this subsection terminates upon the death of the victim.

(c)   Duty in Case of Abuse or Neglect. - Nothing in this section shall be construed to relieve any person of any duty pertaining to abuse or neglect of a child or disabled adult as required by law. (2001-277, s. 1.)

§ 8-53.13. Nurse privilege.

No person licensed pursuant to Article 9A of Chapter 90 of the General Statutes shall be required to disclose any information that may have been acquired in rendering professional nursing services, and which information was necessary to enable that person to render professional nursing services, except that the presiding judge of a superior or district court may compel disclosure if, in the court's opinion, disclosure is necessary to a proper administration of justice and disclosure is not prohibited by other statute or rule. Nothing in this section shall preclude the admission of otherwise admissible written or printed medical records in any judicial proceeding, in accordance with the procedure set forth in G.S. 8-44.1, after a determination by the court that disclosure should be compelled as set forth herein. (2003-342, s. 1; 2004-186, s. 16.1.)

§ 8-54. Defendant in criminal action competent but not compellable to testify.

In the trial of all indictments, complaints, or other proceedings against persons charged with the commission of crimes, offenses or misdemeanors, the person so charged is, at his own request, but not otherwise, a competent witness, and his failure to make such request shall not create any presumption against him. But every such person examined as a witness shall be subject to cross-examination as other witnesses. Except as above provided, nothing in this section shall render any person, who in any criminal proceeding is charged with the commission of a criminal offense, competent or compellable to give evidence against himself, nor render any person compellable to answer any question tending to criminate himself. (1856-7, c. 23; 1866, c. 43, s. 3; 1868-9, c. 209, s. 4; 1881, c. 89, s. 3; c. 110, ss. 2, 3; Code ss. 1353, 1354; Rev., ss. 1634, 1635; C.S., s. 1799.)

§ 8-55. Testimony enforced in certain criminal investigations; immunity.

If any justice, judge or magistrate of the General Court of Justice shall have good reason to believe that any person within his jurisdiction has knowledge of the existence and establishment of any faro bank, faro table or other gaming table prohibited by law, or of any place where alcoholic beverages are sold contrary to law, in any town or county within his jurisdiction, such person not being minded to make voluntary information thereof on oath, then it shall be lawful for such justice, magistrate, or judge to issue to the sheriff of the county in which such faro bank, faro table, gaming table, or place where alcoholic beverages are sold contrary to law is supposed to be a subpoena, capias ad testificandum, or other summons in writing, commanding such person to appear immediately before such justice, magistrate, or judge and give evidence on oath as to what he may know touching the existence, establishment and whereabouts of such faro bank, faro table or other gaming table, or place where alcoholic beverages are sold contrary to law, and the name and personal description of the keeper thereof. Such evidence, when obtained, shall be considered and held in law as an information on oath, and the justice, magistrate or judge may thereupon proceed to seize and arrest such keeper and destroy such table, or issue process therefor as provided by law. No person shall be excused, on any prosecution, from testifying touching any unlawful gaming done by himself or others; but no discovery made by the witness upon such examination shall be used against him in any penal or criminal prosecution, and he shall be altogether pardoned of the offenses so done or participated in by him. (R.C., c. 35, s. 50; 1858-9, c. 34, s. 1; Code, ss. 1050, 1215; 1889, c. 355; Rev., ss. 1637, 3721; 1913, c. 141; C.S., s. 1800; 1969, c. 44, s. 22; 1971, c. 381, s. 4; 1981, c. 412, s. 4(4); c. 747, s. 66.)

§ 8-56. Husband and wife as witnesses in civil action.

In any trial or inquiry in any suit, action or proceeding in any court, or before any person having, by law or consent of parties, authority to examine witnesses or hear evidence, the husband or wife of any party thereto, or of any person in whose behalf any such suit, action or proceeding is brought, prosecuted, opposed or defended, shall, except as herein stated, be competent and compellable to give evidence, as any other witness on behalf of any party to such suit, action or proceeding. No husband or wife shall be compellable to disclose any confidential communication made by one to the other during their marriage. (1866, c. 43, ss. 3, 4; C.C.P., s. 341; Code, s. 588; Rev., s. 1636; 1919, c. 18; C.S., s. 1801; 1945, c. 635; 1977, c. 547; 1983 (Reg. Sess., 1984), c. 1037, s. 3.)

§ 8-57. Husband and wife as witnesses in criminal actions.

(a)   The spouse of the defendant shall be a competent witness for the defendant in all criminal actions, but the failure of the defendant to call such spouse as a witness shall not be used against him. Such spouse is subject to cross-examination as are other witnesses.

(b)   The spouse of the defendant shall be competent but not compellable to testify for the State against the defendant in any criminal action or grand jury proceedings, except that the spouse of the defendant shall be both competent and compellable to so testify:

(1)   In a prosecution for bigamy or criminal cohabitation, to prove the fact of marriage and facts tending to show the absence of divorce or annulment;

(2)   In a prosecution for assaulting or communicating a threat to the other spouse;

(3) In a prosecution for trespass in or upon the separate lands or residence of the other spouse when living separate and apart from each other by mutual consent or court order;

(4) In a prosecution for abandonment of or failure to provide support for the other spouse or their child;

(5) In a prosecution of one spouse for any other criminal offense against the minor child of either spouse, including any child of either spouse who is born out of wedlock or adopted or a foster child.

(c) No husband or wife shall be compellable in any event to disclose any confidential communication made by one to the other during their marriage. (1856-7, c. 23; 1866, c. 43; 1868-9, c. 209; 1881, c. 110; Code, ss. 588, 1353, 1354; Rev., ss. 1634, 1635, 1636; C.S., s. 1802; 1933, c. 13, s. 1; c. 361; 1951, c. 296; 1957, c. 1036; 1967, c. 116; 1971, c. 800; 1973, c. 1286, s. 11; 1983, c. 170, s. 1; 1985 (Reg. Sess., 1986), c. 843, s. 5; 1987 (Reg. Sess., 1988), c. 1040, s. 1; 1989 (Reg. Sess., 1990), c. 1039, s. 4; 1991, c, 686, s. 3; 2013-198, s. 2.)

§ 8-57.1. Husband-wife privilege waived in child abuse.

Notwithstanding the provisions of G.S. 8-56 and G.S. 8-57, the husband-wife privilege shall not be ground for excluding evidence regarding the abuse or neglect of a child under the age of 16 years or regarding an illness of or injuries to such child or the cause thereof in any judicial proceeding related to a report pursuant to the Child Abuse Reporting Law, Article 3 of Chapter 7B of the General Statutes of North Carolina. (1971, c. 710, s. 3; 1998-202, s. 13(d).)

§ 8-57.2. Presumed father or mother as witnesses where paternity at issue.

Whenever an issue of paternity of a child born or conceived during a marriage arises in any civil or criminal proceeding, the presumed father or the mother of such child is competent to give evidence as to any relevant matter regarding paternity of the child, including nonaccess to the present or former spouse, regardless of any privilege which may otherwise apply. No parent offering such evidence shall thereafter be prosecuted based upon that evidence for any criminal act involved in the conception of the child whose paternity is in issue and/or for whom support is sought, except for perjury committed in this testimony. (1981, c. 634, s. 1.)

§ 8-58: Repealed by Session Laws 1973, c. 1286, ss. 11, 26.

§ 8-58.1. Injured party as witness when medical charges at issue.

(a) Whenever an issue of hospital, medical, dental, pharmaceutical, or funeral charges arises in any civil proceeding, the injured party or his guardian, administrator, or executor is competent to give evidence regarding the amount paid or required to be paid in full satisfaction of such charges, provided that records or copies of such charges showing the amount paid or required to be paid in full satisfaction of such charges accompany such testimony.

(b) The testimony of a person pursuant to subsection (a) of this section establishes a rebuttable presumption of the reasonableness of the amount paid or required to be paid in full satisfaction of the charges. However, in the event that the provider of hospital, medical, dental, pharmaceutical, or funeral services gives sworn testimony that the charge for that provider's service either was satisfied by payment of an amount less than the amount charged, or can be satisfied by payment of an amount less than the amount charged, then with respect to that provider's charge only, the presumption of the reasonableness of the amount charged is rebutted and a rebuttable presumption is established that the lesser satisfaction amount is the reasonable amount of the charges for the testifying provider's services. For the purposes of this subsection, the word "provider" shall include the agent or employee of a provider of hospital, medical, dental, pharmaceutical, or funeral services, or a person with responsibility to pay a provider of hospital, medical, dental, pharmaceutical, or funeral services on behalf of an injured party.

(c) The fact that a provider charged for services provided to the injured person establishes a permissive presumption that the services provided were reasonably necessary but no presumption is established that the services provided were necessary because of injuries caused by the acts or omissions of an alleged tortfeasor. (1983, c. 776, s. 1; 2011-283, s. 1.2; 2011-317, s. 1.1.)

§ 8-58.2. Reserved for future codification purposes.

§ 8-58.3. Reserved for future codification purposes.

§ 8-58.4. Reserved for future codification purposes.

§ 8-58.5. Reserved for future codification purposes.

Article 7A.

Restrictions on Evidence in Rape Cases.

§§ 8-58.6 through 8-58.11: Repealed by Session Laws 1983 (Regular Session, 1984), c. 1037, s. 2.

Article 7B.

Expert Testimony.

§§ 8-58.12 through 8-58.14: Repealed by Session Laws 1983 (Regular Session, 1984), c. 1037, s. 9.

§ 8-58.15 through 8-58.19: Reserved for future codification purposes.

Article 7C.

Admissibility of Forensic Evidence.

§ 8-58.20. Forensic analysis admissible as evidence.

(a) In any criminal prosecution, a laboratory report of a written forensic analysis, including an analysis of the defendant's DNA, or a forensic sample alleged to be the defendant's DNA, as that term is defined in G.S. 15A-266.2(2), that states the results of the analysis and that is signed and sworn to by the person performing the analysis may be admissible in evidence without the testimony of the analyst who prepared the report in accordance with the requirements of this section.

(b) A forensic analysis, to be admissible under this section, shall be performed by a laboratory that is accredited by an accrediting body that requires conformance to forensic specific requirements and which is a signatory to the International Laboratory Accreditation Cooperation (ILAC) Mutual Recognition Arrangement For Testing for the submission, identification, analysis, and storage of forensic analyses. The analyses of DNA samples and typing results of DNA samples shall be performed by a laboratory that is accredited by an accrediting body that requires conformance to forensic specific requirements and which is a signatory to the ILAC Mutual Recognition Arrangement For Testing.

(c) The analyst who analyzes the forensic sample and signs the report shall complete an affidavit on a form developed by the State Bureau of Investigation. In the affidavit, the analyst shall state (i) that the person is qualified by education, training, and experience to perform the analysis, (ii) the name and location of the laboratory where the analysis was performed, and (iii) that performing the analysis is part of that person's regular duties. The analyst shall also aver in the affidavit that the tests were performed pursuant to the accrediting body's standards for that discipline and that the evidence was handled in accordance with established and accepted procedures while in the custody of the laboratory. The affidavit shall be sufficient to constitute prima facie evidence regarding the person's qualifications. The analyst shall attach the affidavit to the laboratory report and shall provide the affidavit to the investigating officer and the district attorney in the prosecutorial district in which the criminal charges are pending. An affidavit by a forensic analyst sworn to and properly executed before an official authorized to administer oaths is admissible in evidence without further authentication in any criminal proceeding with respect to the forensic analysis administered and the procedures followed.

(d) The district attorney shall serve a copy of the laboratory report and affidavit and indicate whether the report and affidavit will be offered as evidence at any proceeding against the defendant on the attorney of record for the defendant, or on the defendant if that person has no attorney, no later than five business days after receiving the report and affidavit, or 30 business days before any proceeding in which the report may be used against the defendant, whichever occurs first.

(e) Upon receipt of a copy of the laboratory report and affidavit, the attorney of record for the defendant or the defendant if that person has no attorney, shall have 15 business days to file a written objection to the use of the laboratory report and affidavit at any proceeding against the defendant. The written objection shall be filed with the court in which the matter is pending with a copy provided to the district attorney.

(f)   If the defendant's attorney of record, or the defendant if that person has no attorney, fails to file a written objection with the court to the use of the laboratory report and affidavit within the time allowed by this section, then the laboratory report and affidavit shall be admitted in evidence in any proceeding without the testimony of the analyst subject to the presiding judge ruling otherwise at the proceeding when offered. If, however, a written objection is filed, this section does not apply and the admissibility of the evidence shall be determined and governed by the appropriate rules of evidence.

(g)   Procedure for Establishing Chain of Custody of Evidence Subject to Forensic Analysis Without Calling Unnecessary Witnesses. -

(1)   For the purpose of establishing the chain of physical custody or control of evidence that has been subjected to forensic analysis performed as provided in subsection (b) of this section, a statement signed by each successive person in the chain of custody that the person delivered it to the other person indicated on or about the date stated is prima facie evidence that the person had custody and made the delivery as stated, without the necessity of a personal appearance in court by the person signing the statement.

(2)   The statement shall contain a sufficient description of the material or its container so as to distinguish it as the particular item in question and shall state that the material was delivered in essentially the same condition as received. The statement may be placed on the same document as the report provided for in subsection (a) of this section.

(3)   The provisions of this subsection may be utilized by the State only if (i) the State notifies the defendant at least 15 business days before any proceeding at which the statement would be used of its intention to introduce the statement into evidence under this subsection and provides the defendant with a copy of the statement and (ii) the defendant fails to file a written notification with the court, with a copy to the State, at least five business days before the proceeding that the defendant objects to the introduction of the statement into evidence.

(4)   In lieu of the notice required in subdivision (3) of this subsection, the State may include the statement with the laboratory report and affidavit, as provided in subsection (d) of this section.

(5) If the defendant's attorney of record, or the defendant if that person has no attorney, fails to file the written objection as provided in this subsection, then the statement shall be admitted into evidence without the necessity of a personal appearance by the person signing the statement.

(6) Upon filing a timely objection, the admissibility of the statement shall be determined and governed by the appropriate rules of evidence.

Nothing in this subsection precludes the right of any party to call any witness or to introduce any evidence supporting or contradicting the evidence contained in the statement.

(h) This section does not apply to chemical analyses under G.S. 20-139.1. (2004-124, s. 15.2(c); 2007-484, s. 1; 2009-473, s. 7; 2011-19, s. 7; 2011-307, s. 9; 2012-168, s. 6; 2013-171, ss. 2, 3; 2013-194, s. 2; 2013-338, s. 1.)

Article 8.

Attendance of Witness.

§ 8-59. Issue and service of subpoena.

In obtaining the testimony of witnesses in causes pending in the trial divisions of the General Court of Justice, subpoenas shall be issued and served in the manner provided in Rule 45 of the Rules of Civil Procedure for civil actions. Provided that in criminal cases any employee of a local law-enforcement agency may effect service of a subpoena for the attendance of witnesses by telephone communication with the person named. However, in the case of a witness served by telephone communication pursuant to this section, neither an order to show cause nor an order for arrest shall be issued until such person has been served personally with the written subpoena. (1777, c. 115, s. 36, P.R.; R.C., c. 31, s. 59; Code, s. 1355; Rev., s. 1639; C.S., s. 1803; 1959, c. 522, s. 2; 1967, c. 954, s. 3; 1971, c. 381, s. 5; 1981, c. 267; 1989, c. 262, s. 2.)

§ 8-60. Repealed by Session Laws 1967, c. 954, s. 4.

§ 8-61. Subpoena for the production of documentary evidence.

Subpoenas for the production of records, books, papers, documents, or tangible things may be issued in criminal actions in the same manner as provided for civil actions in Rule 45 of the Rules of Civil Procedure. (1797, c. 476, P.R.; R.C., c. 31, s. 81; Code, s. 1372; Rev., s. 1641; C.S., s. 1805; 1967, c. 954, s. 3; c. 1168.)

§ 8-62. Repealed by Session Laws 1967, c. 954, s. 4.

§ 8-63. Witnesses attend until discharge; effect of nonattendance.

Every witness, being summoned to appear in any of the said courts, in manner before directed, shall appear accordingly, and, subject to the provisions of G.S. 6-51, continue to attend from session to session until discharged, when summoned in a civil action or special proceeding, by the court or the party at whose instance such witness shall be summoned, or, when summoned in a criminal prosecution, until discharged by the court, the prosecuting officer, or the party at whose instance he was summoned; and in default thereof shall forfeit and pay, in civil actions or special proceedings, to the party at whose instance the subpoena issued, the sum of forty dollars ($40.00), to be recovered by motion in the cause, and shall be further liable to his action for the full damages which may be sustained for the want of such witness's testimony; or if summoned in a criminal prosecution shall forfeit and pay eighty dollars ($80.00) for the use of the State, or the party summoning him. If the civil action or special proceeding shall, in the vacation, be compromised and settled between the parties, and the party at whose instance such witness was summoned should omit to discharge him from further attendance, and for want of such discharge he shall attend the next session, in that case the witness, upon oath made of the facts, shall be entitled to a ticket from the clerk in the same manner as other witnesses, and shall recover from the party at whose instance he was summoned the allowance which is given to witnesses for their attendance, with costs.

No execution shall issue against any defaulting witness for the forfeiture aforesaid but after notice made known to him to show cause against the issuing thereof; and if sufficient cause be shown of his incapacity to attend, execution shall not issue, and the witness shall be discharged of the forfeiture without costs; but otherwise the court shall, on motion, award execution for the forfeiture against the defaulting witness. (1777, c. 115, ss. 37, 38, 43, P.R.; 1799, c. 528,

P.R.; 1801, c. 591, P.R.; R.C., c. 31, ss. 60, 61, 62; Code, s. 1356; Rev., s. 1643; C.S., s. 1807; 1965, c. 284; 1971, c. 381, s. 12.)

§ 8-64. Witnesses exempt from civil arrest.

Every witness shall be exempt from arrest in civil actions or special proceedings during his attendance at any court, or before a commissioner, arbitrator, referee, or other person authorized to command the attendance of such witness, and during the time such witness is going to and returning from the place of such attendance, allowing one day for every thirty miles such witness has to travel to and from his place of residence. (1777, c. 115, s. 44, P.R.; R.C., c. 31, s. 70; Code, s. 1367; Rev., s. 1644; C.S., s. 1808.)

Article 9.

Attendance of Witnesses from without State.

§§ 8-65 through 8-70. Transferred to §§ 15A-811 through 15A-816 by Session Laws 1973, c. 1286, s. 9.

Article 10.

Depositions.

§§ 8-71 through 8-73. Repealed by Session Laws 1967, c. 954, s. 4.

§ 8-74. Depositions for defendant in criminal actions.

In all criminal actions, hearings and investigations it shall be lawful for the defendant in any such action to make affidavit before the clerk of the superior court of the county in which said action is pending, that it is important for the defense that he have the testimony of any person, whose name must be given, and that such person is so infirm, or otherwise physically incapacitated, or nonresident of this State, that he cannot procure his attendance at the trial or hearing of said cause. Upon the filing of such affidavit, it shall be the duty of the clerk to appoint some responsible person to take the deposition of such witness, which deposition may be read in the trial of such criminal action under the same rules as now apply by law to depositions in civil actions: provided, that the district attorney or prosecuting attorney of the district, county or town in which such action is pending have 10 days' notice of the taking of such deposition, who may appear in person or by representative to conduct the cross-examination of such witness. (Code, s. 1357; 1891, c. 522; 1893, c. 80; Rev., s. 1652; 1915, c. 251; C.S., s. 1812; 1971, c. 381, s. 6; 1973, c. 47, s. 2.)

§ 8-75. Repealed by Session Laws 1971, c. 381, s. 13.

§ 8-76. Depositions before municipal authorities.

Any board of aldermen, board of town or county commissioners or any person interested in any proceeding, investigation, hearing or trial before such board, may take the depositions of all persons whose evidence may be desired for use in said proceeding, investigation, hearing or trial; and to do so, the chairman of such board or such person may apply in person or by attorney to the superior court clerk of that county in which such proceeding, investigation, hearing or trial is pending, for a commission to take the same, and said clerk, upon such application, shall issue such commission, or such deposition may be taken by a notary public of this State or of any other state or foreign country without a commission issuing from the court; and the notice and proceedings upon the taking of said depositions shall be the same as provided for in civil actions; and if the person upon whom the notice of the taking of such deposition is to be served is absent from or cannot after due diligence be found within this State, but can be found within the county in which the deposition is to be taken, then, and in that case, said notice shall be personally served on such person by the commissioner appointed to take such deposition or by the notary taking such deposition, as the case may be; and when any such deposition is returned to the clerk it shall be opened and passed upon by him and delivered to such board, and the reading and using of such deposition shall conform to the rules of the superior court. (1889, c. 151; Rev., s. 1653; C.S., s. 1814; 1943, c. 543.)

§ 8-77: Repealed by Session Laws 1995, c. 379, s. 9.

§ 8-78. Commissioner may subpoena witness and punish for contempt.

Commissioners to take depositions appointed by the courts of this State, or by the courts of the states or territories of the United States, arbitrators, referees, and all persons acting under a commission issuing from any court of record in this State, are hereby empowered, they or the clerks of the courts respectively in this State, to which such commission shall be returnable, to issue subpoenas, specifying the time and place for the attendance of witnesses before them, and to administer oaths to said witnesses, to the end that they may give their testimony. And any witness appearing before any of the said persons and refusing to give his testimony on oath touching such matters as he may be lawfully examined unto shall be committed, by warrant of the person before whom he shall so refuse, to the common jail of the county, there to remain until he may be willing to give his evidence; which warrant of commitment shall recite what authority the person has to take the testimony of such witness, and the refusal of the witness to give it. (1777, c. 115, s. 42, P.R.; 1805, c. 685, ss. 1, 2, P.R.; 1848, c. 66; 1850, c. 188; R.C., c. 31, s. 64; Code, s. 1362; Rev., s. 1649; C.S., s. 1816.)

§ 8-79. Attendance before commissioner enforced.

The sheriff of the county where the witness may be shall execute all such subpoenas, and make due return thereof before the commissioner, or other person, before whom the witness is to appear, in the same manner, and under the same penalties, as in case of process of a like kind returnable to court; and when the witness shall be subpoenaed five days before the time of his required attendance, and shall fail to appear according to the subpoena and give evidence, the default shall be noted by the commissioner, arbitrator, or other person aforesaid; and in case the default be made before a commissioner acting under authority from courts without the State, the defaulting witness shall forfeit and pay to the party at whose instance he may be subpoenaed fifty dollars, and on the trial for such penalty the subpoena issued by the commissioner, or other person, as aforesaid, with the indorsement thereon of due service by the officer serving the same, together with the default noted as aforesaid and indorsed on the subpoena, shall be prima facie evidence of the forfeiture, and sufficient to entitle the plaintiff to judgment for the same, unless the witness may show his incapacity to have attended. (1848, c. 66, s. 2; 1850, c. 188, ss. 1, 2; R.C., c. 31, s. 65; Code, s. 1363; Rev., s. 1650; C.S., s. 1817.)

§ 8-80. Remedies against defaulting witness before commissioner.

But in case the default be made before a commissioner, arbitrator, referee or other person, acting under a commission or authority from any of the courts of this State, then the same shall be certified under his hand, and returned with the subpoena to the court by which he was commissioned or empowered to take the evidence of such witness; and thereupon the court shall adjudge the defaulting witness to pay to the party at whose instance he was summoned the sum of forty dollars ($40.00); but execution shall not issue therefor until the same be ordered by the court, after such proceedings had as shall give said witness an opportunity to show cause, if he can, against the issuing thereof. (1850, c. 188, s. 2; R.C., c. 31, s. 66; Code, s. 1364; Rev., s. 1651; C.S., s. 1818.)

§ 8-81. Objection to deposition before trial.

At any time before the trial, or hearing of an action or proceeding, any party may make a motion to the judge or court to reject a deposition for irregularity in the taking of it, either in whole or in part, for scandal, impertinence, the incompetency of the testimony, for insufficient notice, or for any other good cause. The objecting party shall state his exceptions in writing. (1869-70, c. 227, ss. 13, 17; Code, s. 1361; 1895, c. 312; 1903, c. 132; Rev., s. 1648; C.S., s. 1819.)

§ 8-82. Deposition not quashed after trial begun.

No deposition shall be quashed, or rejected, on objection first made after a trial has begun, merely because of an irregularity in taking the same, provided it shall appear that the party objecting had notice that it had been taken, and it was on file long enough before the trial to enable him to present his objection. (1869-70, c. 227, s. 12; Code, s. 1360; Rev., s. 1647; C.S., s. 1820.)

§ 8-83. When deposition may be read on the trial.

Every deposition taken and returned in the manner provided by law may be read on the trial of the action or proceeding, or before any referee, in the following cases, and not otherwise:

(1)   If the witness is dead, or has become insane since the deposition was taken.

(2) If the witness is a resident of a foreign country, or of another state, and is not present at the trial.

(3) If the witness is confined in a prison outside the county in which the trial takes place.

(4) If the witness is so old, sick or infirm as to be unable to attend court.

(5) If the witness is the President of the United States, or the head of any department of the federal government, or a judge, district attorney, or clerk of any court of the United States, and the trial shall take place during the term of such court.

(6) If the witness is the Governor of the State, or the head of any department of the State government, or the president of the University, or the head of any other incorporated college in the State, or the superintendent or any physician in the employ of any of the hospitals for the insane for the State.

(7) If the witness is a justice of the Supreme Court, judge of the Court of Appeals, or a judge, presiding officer, clerk or district attorney of any court of record, and the trial shall take place during the term of such court.

(8) If the witness is a member of the Congress of the United States, or a member of the General Assembly, and the trial shall take place during a time that such member is in the service of that body.

(9) Except in actions or proceedings governed by the Rules of Civil Procedure, if the witness has been duly summoned, and at the time of the trial is out of the State, or is more than seventy-five miles by the usual public mode of travel from the place where the court is sitting, without the procurement or consent of the party offering his deposition.

(10) If the action is pending in a magistrate's court the deposition may be read on the trial of the action, provided the witness is more than 75 miles by the usual public mode of travel from the place where the court is sitting.

(11) Except in actions or proceedings governed by the Rules of Civil Procedure, if the witness is a physician duly licensed to practice medicine in the State of North Carolina, and resides or maintains his office outside the county in which the action is pending.

If any provision of this section conflicts with the Rules of Civil Procedure, then those Rules shall control in actions or proceedings governed by them. (1777, c. 115, ss. 39, 40, 41, P.R.; 1803, c. 633, P.R.; 1828, ch. 24, ss. 1, 2; 1836, c. 30; R.C., c. 31, s. 63; 1869-70, c. 227, s. 11; 1881, c. 279, ss. 1, 3; Code, s. 1358; 1905, c. 366; Rev., s. 1645; 1919, c. 324; C.S., s. 1821; 1965, c. 675; 1969, c. 44, s. 23; 1971, c. 381, s. 7; 1973, c. 47, s. 2; 1991, c. 491, s. 1.)

§ 8-84. Repealed by Session Laws 1975, c. 762, s. 4.

Article 11.

Perpetuation of Testimony.

§ 8-85. Court reporter's certified transcription.

Testimony taken and transcribed by a court reporter and certified by the reporter or by the judge who presided at the trial at which the testimony was given, may be offered in evidence in any court as the deposition of the witness whose testimony is so taken and transcribed, in the manner, and under the rules governing the introduction of depositions in civil actions. (1971, c. 377, s. 1.)

§§ 8-86 through 8-88. Repealed by Session Laws 1967, c. 954, s. 4.

Article 12.

Inspection and Production of Writings.

§ 8-89. Repealed by Session Laws 1967, c. 954, s. 4.

§ 8-89.1. Repealed by Session Laws 1975, c. 762, s. 4.

§§ 8-90 through 8-91. Repealed by Session Laws 1967, c. 954, s. 4.

§ 8-92. Reserved for future codification purposes.

§ 8-93. Reserved for future codification purposes.

§ 8-94. Reserved for future codification purposes.

§ 8-95. Reserved for future codification purposes.

§ 8-96. Reserved for future codification purposes.

Article 13.

Photographs.

§ 8-97. Photographs as substantive or illustrative evidence.

Any party may introduce a photograph, video tape, motion picture, X-ray or other photographic representation as substantive evidence upon laying a proper foundation and meeting other applicable evidentiary requirements. This section does not prohibit a party from introducing a photograph or other pictorial representation solely for the purpose of illustrating the testimony of a witness. (1981, c. 451, s. 1.)

§ 8-98. Reserved for future codification purposes.

§ 8-99. Reserved for future codification purposes.

§ 8-100. Reserved for future codification purposes.

§ 8-101. Reserved for future codification purposes.

§ 8-102. Reserved for future codification purposes.

Chapter 14.

Chain of Custody.

§ 8-103. Courier service and contract carriers.

For purposes of maintaining a chain of custody for any item of evidence, depositing the item with the State courier service operated by the Department of Administration or a common or contract carrier shall be considered the same as depositing such item in first class United States mail. (1983, c. 375, s. 1.)

§ 8-104. Reserved for future codification purposes.

§ 8-105. Reserved for future codification purposes.

§ 8-106. Reserved for future codification purposes.

§ 8-107. Reserved for future codification purposes.

§ 8-108. Reserved for future codification purposes.

§ 8-109. Reserved for future codification purposes.

Article 15.

Mediation Negotiations.

§ 8-110. Inadmissibility of negotiations.

(a) Evidence of statements made and conduct occurring during mediation at a community mediation center authorized by G.S. 7A-38.5 shall not be subject to discovery and shall be inadmissible in any proceeding in the action or other actions on the same claim, except in proceedings to enforce a settlement of the action. No such settlement shall be binding unless it has been reduced to writing and signed by the parties. No evidence otherwise discoverable shall be inadmissible merely because it is presented or discussed during mediation.

(b) No mediator shall be compelled to testify or produce evidence in any civil proceeding concerning statements made and conduct occurring in a mediation conducted by a community mediation center authorized by G.S. 7A-38.5. A civil proceeding includes any civil matter in any administrative agency or the General Court of Justice, including a proceeding to enforce a settlement reached at the mediation. For purposes of this subsection, a mediator is a person assigned by the center to conduct the mediation and any staff person employed by the center to provide supervision of that person. This subsection does not excuse a mediator from the reporting requirements of G.S. 7B-301 or G.S. 108A-102.

(c)   Except as provided in this subsection, no mediator shall be compelled to testify or produce evidence in any criminal misdemeanor or felony proceeding concerning statements made and conduct occurring in a mediation conducted at a community mediation center authorized by G.S. 7A-38.5. A judge presiding over the trial of a felony may, however, compel disclosure of any evidence unrelated to the dispute that is the subject of the mediation if it is to be introduced in the trial or disposition of the felony and the judge determines that the introduction of the evidence is necessary to a proper administration of justice, and the evidence may not be obtained from any other source. For purposes of this subsection, a mediator is a person assigned by the center to conduct the mediation and any staff person employed by the center to provide supervision of that person. This subsection does not excuse a mediator from the reporting requirements of G.S. 7B-301 or G.S. 108A-102. (1999-354, s. 4.)

Chapter 8A.

Interpreters for Deaf Persons.

§ 8A-1. Recodified as §§ 8B-1 to 8B-9.

Chapter 8B.

Interpreters for Deaf Persons.

§ 8B-1. Definitions; right to interpreter; determination of competence.

As used in this Chapter:

(1)   "Appointing authority" means the presiding judge or clerk of superior court in a judicial proceeding, or a hearing officer, examiner, commissioner, chairman, presiding officer or similar official in a legislative or administrative proceeding.

(2)   "Deaf person" means a person whose hearing impairment is so significant that the individual is impaired in processing linguistic information through hearing, with or without amplification.

(3) "Qualified interpreter" means an interpreter licensed under Chapter 90D of the General Statutes. If the appointing authority finds that a licensed interpreter is not available, an unlicensed interpreter may be called and used as a qualified interpreter if the interpreter's actual qualifications have otherwise been determined to be adequate for the present need. In no event will an interpreter be considered qualified if the interpreter is unable to communicate effectively with and simultaneously and accurately interpret for the deaf person.

A deaf person who does not utilize sign language may request an aural/oral interpreter. Before this interpreter is appointed, the appointing authority shall satisfy itself that the aural/oral interpreter is competent to interpret the proceedings to the deaf person and to present the testimony, statements, and any other information tendered by the deaf person. (1981, c. 937, s. 1; 1997-443, s. 11A.118(a); 2002-182, s. 2; 2003-56, s. 3.)

§ 8B-2. Appointment of interpreters in certain judicial, legislative, and administrative proceedings; removal.

(a) When a deaf person is a party to or a witness in any civil or criminal proceeding in any superior or district court of the State, including juvenile proceedings, special proceedings, and proceedings before the magistrate, the court shall appoint a qualified interpreter to interpret the proceedings to the deaf person and to interpret the deaf person's testimony, if any.

(b) When a deaf person is a witness before any legislative committee or subcommittee or legislative research or study committee or subcommittee or commission authorized by the General Assembly, the appointing authority conducting the proceeding shall appoint a qualified interpreter to interpret the proceedings to the deaf person and to interpret the deaf person's testimony.

(c) When a deaf person is a party to or a witness in an administrative proceeding before any department, board, commission, agency or licensing authority of the State, or of any county or city of the State, the appointing authority conducting the proceeding shall appoint a qualified interpreter to interpret the proceedings to the deaf person and to interpret the deaf person's testimony, if any.

(d) If a deaf person is arrested for an alleged violation of criminal law of the State, including a local ordinance, the arresting officer shall immediately procure a qualified interpreter from the appropriate court for any interrogation, warning, notification of rights, arraignment, bail hearing or other preliminary proceeding, but no arrestee otherwise eligible for release on bail under Article 26 of Chapter 15A of the General Statutes shall be held in custody pending the arrival of an interpreter. No answer, statement or admission taken from the deaf person without a qualified interpreter present and functioning is admissible in court for any purpose.

(e) Whenever a juvenile whose parent or parents are deaf is brought before a court for any reason whatsoever, the court shall appoint a qualified interpreter to interpret the proceedings and testimony for the deaf parent or parents, and to interpret any statements or testimony the deaf parent or parents may be called upon to give to the court.

(f) A qualified interpreter shall not be appointed until the appointing authority makes a preliminary determination that the interpreter is able to communicate effectively with and to interpret accurately for the deaf person. If no qualified interpreter can be found who can successfully communicate with this person, he may select his own interpreter without regard to whether the interpreter is "qualified" within the meaning set forth under this statute.

(g) The appointing authority may, on its own motion or on the request of the deaf person, remove an interpreter for inability to communicate or because his services have been waived. (1981, c. 937, s. 1.)

§ 8B-3. Waiver of appointed interpreter.

(a) A deaf person entitled to the services of an interpreter under this Chapter may waive these services. The waiver must be approved in writing by the person's attorney. If the person does not have an attorney, approval must be made in writing by the appointing authority.

(b) A deaf person who has waived an interpreter under this section may provide his own interpreter at his own expense, without regard to whether such interpreter is qualified under this Chapter. (1981, c. 937, s. 1.)

§ 8B-4. Notice of need for interpreter; proof of deafness.

A deaf person entitled to an interpreter under this Chapter shall, if practicable, notify the appropriate appointing authority of his need prior to his appearance. A failure to notify or to request an interpreter is not a waiver of the right to an interpreter. Before appointing an interpreter, an appointing authority may require satisfactory proof of the requesting person's deafness if he has reason to believe the person is not hearing impaired. (1981, c. 937, s. 1.)

§ 8B-5. Privileged communications.

If a communication made by the deaf person through an interpreter is privileged, the privilege extends also to the interpreter. (1981, c. 937, s. 1.)

§ 8B-6. List of interpreters; coordination of interpreter services.

The Department of Health and Human Services shall prepare and maintain an up-to-date list of qualified and available interpreters. A copy of the list shall be provided to each clerk of superior court and to the North Carolina Interpreter and Transliterator Licensing Board created in Chapter 90D of the General Statutes. When requested by an appointing authority to provide an interpreter the Division of Services for the Deaf and the Hard of Hearing shall assist in arranging for an interpreter at the time and place needed through its program of community services for the hearing impaired. (1981, c. 937, s. 1; 1989, c. 533, s. 4; 1997-443, s. 11A.118(a); 2002-182, s. 3; 2003-56, s. 3.)

§ 8B-7. Oath.

Before acting, an interpreter shall take an oath or affirmation that he will make a true interpretation in an understandable manner of the proceedings to the person for whom he is appointed and that he will convey the statements of the person in the English language to the best of his skill and judgment. (1981, c. 937, s. 1.)

§ 8B-8. Compensation.

(a)   An interpreter appointed under this Chapter is entitled to a reasonable fee for services, including waiting time, time reserved by the courts for the assignment, and reimbursement for necessary travel and subsistence expenses. The fee shall be fixed by the appointing authority who shall consider any fee schedule for interpreters established by the Department of Health and

Human Services. Reimbursement for necessary travel and subsistence expenses shall be at rates provided by law for State employees generally.

(b) The fees and expenses of interpreters who serve before any superior or district court criminal and juvenile proceeding are payable from funds appropriated to the Administrative Office of the Courts.

(c) The fees and expenses of interpreters who serve in civil cases and special proceedings are also payable from funds appropriated to the Administrative Office of the Courts.

(d) Fees and expenses of interpreters who serve before a legislative body described in this Article are payable from funds appropriated for operating expenses of the General Assembly.

(e) Fees and expenses of interpreters who serve before any State administrative agency are payable by that agency.

(f) Fees and expenses of interpreters who serve before city or county administrative proceedings are payable by the respective city or county.

(g) Repealed by Session Laws 1995, c. 277, s. 1. (1981, c. 937, s. 1; 1989, c. 533, s. 5; 1995, c. 277, s. 1; 1997-443, s. 11A.118(a).)

§ 8B-9. Responsibility for payment of funds to implement Chapter.

Responsibility for payment of funds to implement this Chapter rests with the particular entity specified in G.S. 8B-8 whose procedure required the service. (1981, c. 937, s. 2.)

§ 8B-10. North Carolina Training and Licensing Preparation Program fees.

The Division of Services for the Deaf and the Hard of Hearing of the Department of Health and Human Services may charge a fee of no more than fifty dollars ($50.00) to individuals who participate in interpreter training or workshops offered by the North Carolina Training and Licensing Preparation Program. The Division may charge a fee of no more than one hundred dollars ($100.00) for a diagnostic evaluation offered under the Program. This fee is for voluntary diagnostic services only. These fees are to cover the cost of administering the

Program and are payable when a participant takes part in a planned activity. (1991, c. 465, s. 1; 1997-443, s. 11A.118(a); 2002-182, s. 4; 2003-56, s. 3.)

Chapter 8C.

Evidence Code.

§ 8C-1. Rules of Evidence.

The North Carolina Rules of Evidence are as follows:

Article 1.

General Provisions.

Rule 101. Scope.

These rules govern proceedings in the courts of this State to the extent and with the exceptions stated in Rule 1101. (1983, ch. 701, s. 1.)

Rule 102. Purpose and construction.

(a) In general. - These rules shall be construed to secure fairness in administration, elimination of unjustifiable expense and delay, and promotion of growth and development of the law of evidence to the end that the truth may be ascertained and proceedings justly determined.

(b) Subordinate divisions. - For the purpose of these rules only, the subordinate division of any rule which is labeled with a lower case letter shall be a subdivision. (1983, c. 701, s. 1.)

Rule 103. Rulings on evidence.

(a) Effect of erroneous ruling. - Error may not be predicated upon a ruling which admits or excludes evidence unless a substantial right of the party is affected, and

(1) Objection. - In case the ruling is one admitting evidence, a timely objection or motion to strike appears of record. No particular form is required in order to preserve the right to assert the alleged error upon appeal if the motion or objection clearly presented the alleged error to the trial court;

(2) Offer of proof. - In case the ruling is one excluding evidence, the substance of the evidence was made known to the court by offer or was apparent from the context within which questions were asked.

Once the court makes a definitive ruling on the record admitting or excluding evidence, either at or before trial, a party need not renew an objection or offer of proof to preserve a claim of error for appeal.

(b) Record of offer and ruling. - The court may add any other or further statement which shows the character of the evidence, the form in which it was offered, the objection made, and the ruling thereon. It may direct the making of an offer in question and answer form.

(c) Hearing of jury. - In jury cases, proceedings shall be conducted, to the extent practicable, so as to prevent inadmissible evidence from being suggested to the jury by any means, such as making statements or offers of proof or asking questions in the hearing of the jury.

(d) Review of errors where justice requires. - Notwithstanding the requirements of subdivision (a) of this rule, an appellate court may review errors affecting substantial rights if it determines, in the interest of justice, it is appropriate to do so. (1983, c. 701, s. 1; 2003-101, s. 1; 2006-264, s. 30.5.)

Rule 104. Preliminary questions.

(a) Questions of admissibility generally. - Preliminary questions concerning the qualification of a person to be a witness, the existence of a privilege, or the admissibility of evidence shall be determined by the court, subject to the provisions of subdivision (b). In making its determination it is not bound by the rules of evidence except those with respect to privileges.

(b) Relevancy conditioned on fact. - When the relevancy of evidence depends upon the fulfillment of a condition of fact, the court shall admit it upon, or subject to, the introduction of evidence sufficient to support a finding of the fulfillment of the condition.

(c) Hearing of jury. - Hearings on the admissibility of confessions or other motions to suppress evidence in criminal trials in Superior Court shall in all cases be conducted out of the hearing of the jury. Hearings on other preliminary matters shall be so conducted when the interests of justice require or, when an accused is a witness, if he so requests.

(d) Testimony by accused. - The accused does not, by testifying upon a preliminary matter, subject himself to cross-examination as to other issues in the case.

(e) Weight and credibility. - This rule does not limit the right of a party to introduce before the jury evidence relevant to weight or credibility. (1983, ch. 701, s. 1.)

Rule 105. Limited admissibility.

When evidence which is admissible as to one party or for one purpose but not admissible as to another party or for another purpose is admitted, the court, upon request, shall restrict the evidence to its proper scope and instruct the jury accordingly. (1983, c. 701, s. 1.)

Rule 106. Remainder of or related writings or recorded statements.

When a writing or recorded statement or part thereof is introduced by a party, an adverse party may require him at that time to introduce any other part or any other writing or recorded statement which ought in fairness to be considered contemporaneously with it. (1983, c. 701, s. 1.)

Article 2.

Judicial Notice.

Rule 201. Judicial notice of adjudicative facts.

(a) Scope of rule. - This rule governs only judicial notice of adjudicative facts.

(b) Kinds of facts. - A judicially noticed fact must be one not subject to reasonable dispute in that it is either (1) generally known within the territorial jurisdiction of the trial court or (2) capable of accurate and ready determination by resort to sources whose accuracy cannot reasonably be questioned.

(c) When discretionary. - A court may take judicial notice, whether requested or not.

(d) When mandatory. - A court shall take judicial notice if requested by a party and supplied with the necessary information.

(e) Opportunity to be heard. - In a trial court, a party is entitled upon timely request to an opportunity to be heard as to the propriety of taking judicial notice and the tenor of the matter noticed. In the absence of prior notification, the request may be made after judicial notice has been taken.

(f) Time of taking notice. - Judicial notice may be taken at any stage of the proceeding.

(g) Instructing jury. - In a civil action or proceeding, the court shall instruct the jury to accept as conclusive any fact judicially noticed. In a criminal case, the court shall instruct the jury that it may, but is not required to, accept as conclusive any fact judicially noticed. (1983, c. 701, s. 1.)

Article 3.

Presumptions in Civil Actions and Proceedings.

Rule 301. Presumptions in general in civil actions and proceedings.

In all civil actions and proceedings when not otherwise provided for by statute, by judicial decision, or by these rules, a presumption imposes on the party against whom it is directed the burden of going forward with evidence to rebut or meet the presumption, but does not shift to such party the burden of proof in the sense of the risk of nonpersuasion, which remains throughout the trial upon the party on whom it was originally cast. The burden of going forward is satisfied by the introduction of evidence sufficient to permit reasonable minds to conclude that the presumed fact does not exist. If the party against whom a presumption operates fails to meet the burden of producing evidence, the presumed fact shall be deemed proved, and the court shall instruct the jury accordingly. When the burden of producing evidence to meet a presumption is satisfied, the court must instruct the jury that it may, but is not required to, infer the existence of the presumed fact from the proved fact. (1983, c. 701, s. 1.)

Rule 302. Applicability of federal law in civil actions and proceedings.

In civil actions and proceedings, the effect of a presumption respecting a fact which is an element of a claim or defense as to which federal law supplies the rule of decision is determined in accordance with federal law. (1983, c. 701, s. 1.)

Article 4.

Relevancy and Its Limits.

Rule 401. Definition of "relevant evidence."

"Relevant evidence" means evidence having any tendency to make the existence of any fact that is of consequence to the determination of the action more probable or less probable than it would be without the evidence. (1983, c. 701, s. 1.)

Rule 402. Relevant evidence generally admissible; irrelevant evidence inadmissible.

All relevant evidence is admissible, except as otherwise provided by the Constitution of the United States, by the Constitution of North Carolina, by Act of Congress, by Act of the General Assembly or by these rules. Evidence which is not relevant is not admissible. (1983, c. 701, s. 1.)

Rule 403. Exclusion of relevant evidence on grounds of prejudice, confusion, or waste of time.

Although relevant, evidence may be excluded if its probative value is substantially outweighed by the danger of unfair prejudice, confusion of the issues, or misleading the jury, or by considerations of undue delay, waste of time, or needless presentation of cumulative evidence. (1983, c. 701, s. 1.)

Rule 404. Character evidence not admissible to prove conduct; exceptions; other crimes.

(a) Character evidence generally. - Evidence of a person's character or a trait of his character is not admissible for the purpose of proving that he acted in conformity therewith on a particular occasion, except:

(1) Character of accused. - Evidence of a pertinent trait of his character offered by an accused, or by the prosecution to rebut the same;

(2) Character of victim. - Evidence of a pertinent trait of character of the victim of the crime offered by an accused, or by the prosecution to rebut the same, or evidence of a character trait of peacefulness of the victim offered by the prosecution in a homicide case to rebut evidence that the victim was the first aggressor;

(3) Character of witness. - Evidence of the character of a witness, as provided in Rules 607, 608, and 609.

(b) Other crimes, wrongs, or acts. - Evidence of other crimes, wrongs, or acts is not admissible to prove the character of a person in order to show that he acted in conformity therewith. It may, however, be admissible for other purposes, such as proof of motive, opportunity, intent, preparation, plan, knowledge, identity, or absence of mistake, entrapment or accident. Admissible evidence may include evidence of an offense committed by a juvenile if it would have been a Class A, B1, B2, C, D, or E felony if committed by an adult. (1983, c. 701, s. 1; 1994, Ex. Sess., c. 7, s. 3; 1995, c. 509, s. 7.)

Rule 405. Methods of proving character.

(a) Reputation or opinion. - In all cases in which evidence of character or a trait of character of a person is admissible, proof may be made by testimony as to reputation or by testimony in the form of an opinion. On cross-examination, inquiry is allowable into relevant specific instances of conduct. Expert testimony on character or a trait of character is not admissible as circumstantial evidence of behavior.

(b) Specific instances of conduct. - In cases in which character or a trait of character of a person is an essential element of a charge, claim, or defense, proof may also be made of specific instances of his conduct. (1983, c. 701, s. 1.)

Rule 406. Habit; routine practice.

Evidence of the habit of a person or of the routine practice of an organization, whether corroborated or not and regardless of the presence of eyewitnesses, is relevant to prove that the conduct of the person or organization on a particular occasion was in conformity with the habit or routine practice. (1983, c. 701, s. 1.)

Rule 407. Subsequent remedial measures.

When, after an event, measures are taken which, if taken previously, would have made the event less likely to occur, evidence of the subsequent measures is not admissible to prove negligence or culpable conduct in connection with the event. This rule does not require the exclusion of evidence of subsequent measures when offered for another purpose, such as proving ownership, control, or feasibility of precautionary measures, if those issues are controverted, or impeachment. (1983, c. 701, s. 1.)

Rule 408. Compromise and offers to compromise.

Evidence of (1) furnishing or offering or promising to furnish, or (2) accepting or offering or promising to accept, a valuable consideration in compromising or attempting to compromise a claim which was disputed as to either validity or amount, is not admissible to prove liability for or invalidity of the claim or its amount. Evidence of conduct or evidence of statements made in compromise negotiations is likewise not admissible. This rule does not require the exclusion of any evidence otherwise discoverable merely because it is presented in the course of compromise negotiations. This rule also does not require exclusion when the evidence is offered for another purpose, such as proving bias or prejudice of a witness, negativing a contention of undue delay, or proving an effort to obstruct a criminal investigation or prosecution. (1983, c. 701, s. 1.)

Rule 409. Payment of medical and other expenses.

Evidence of furnishing or offering or promising to pay medical, hospital, or other expenses occasioned by an injury is not admissible to prove liability for the injury. (1983, c. 701, s. 1.)

Rule 410. Inadmissibility of pleas, plea discussions, and related statements.

Except as otherwise provided in this rule, evidence of the following is not, in any civil or criminal proceeding, admissible for or against the defendant who made the plea or was a participant in the plea discussions:

(1) A plea of guilty which was later withdrawn;

(2) A plea of no contest;

(3) Any statement made in the course of any proceedings under Article 58 of Chapter 15A of the General Statutes or comparable procedure in district court, or proceedings under Rule 11 of the Federal Rules of Criminal Procedure or comparable procedure in another state, regarding a plea of guilty which was later withdrawn or a plea of no contest;

(4) Any statement made in the course of plea discussions with an attorney for the prosecuting authority which do not result in a plea of guilty or which result in a plea of guilty later withdrawn.

However, such a statement is admissible in any proceeding wherein another statement made in the course of the same plea or plea discussions has been introduced and the statement ought in fairness be considered contemporaneously with it. (1983, c. 701, s. 1.)

Rule 411. Liability insurance.

Evidence that a person was or was not insured against liability is not admissible upon the issue whether he acted negligently or otherwise wrongfully. This rule does not require the exclusion of evidence of insurance against liability when offered for another purpose, such as proof of agency, ownership, or control, or bias or prejudice of a witness. (1983, c. 701, s. 1.)

Rule 412. Rape or sex offense cases; relevance of victim's past behavior.

(a)   As used in this rule, the term "sexual behavior" means sexual activity of the complainant other than the sexual act which is at issue in the indictment on trial.

(b)   Notwithstanding any other provision of law, the sexual behavior of the complainant is irrelevant to any issue in the prosecution unless such behavior:

(1)   Was between the complainant and the defendant; or

(2)   Is evidence of specific instances of sexual behavior offered for the purpose of showing that the act or acts charged were not committed by the defendant; or

(3)   Is evidence of a pattern of sexual behavior so distinctive and so closely resembling the defendant's version of the alleged encounter with the complainant as to tend to prove that such complainant consented to the act or acts charged or behaved in such a manner as to lead the defendant reasonably to believe that the complainant consented; or

(4)   Is evidence of sexual behavior offered as the basis of expert psychological or psychiatric opinion that the complainant fantasized or invented the act or acts charged.

(c)   Sexual behavior otherwise admissible under this rule may not be proved by reputation or opinion.

(d)   Notwithstanding any other provision of law, unless and until the court determines that evidence of sexual behavior is relevant under subdivision (b), no reference to this behavior may be made in the presence of the jury and no evidence of this behavior may be introduced at any time during the trial of:

(1)   A charge of rape or a lesser included offense of rape;

(2)   A charge of a sex offense or a lesser included offense of a sex offense; or

(3)   An offense being tried jointly with a charge of rape or a sex offense, or with a lesser included offense of rape or a sex offense.

Before any questions pertaining to such evidence are asked of any witness, the proponent of such evidence shall first apply to the court for a determination of the relevance of the sexual behavior to which it relates. The proponent of such evidence may make application either prior to trial pursuant to G.S. 15A-952, or during the trial at the time when the proponent desires to introduce such evidence. When application is made, the court shall conduct an in camera hearing, which shall be transcribed, to consider the proponent's offer of proof and the argument of counsel, including any counsel for the complainant, to determine the extent to which such behavior is relevant. In the hearing, the proponent of the evidence shall establish the basis of admissibility of such evidence. Notwithstanding subdivision (b) of Rule 104, if the relevancy of the evidence which the proponent seeks to offer in the trial depends upon the fulfillment of a condition of fact, the court, at the in camera hearing or at a subsequent in camera hearing scheduled for that purpose, shall accept evidence on the issue of whether that condition of fact is fulfilled and shall determine that issue. If the court finds that the evidence is relevant, it shall enter an order stating that the evidence may be admitted and the nature of the questions which will be permitted.

(e)   The record of the in camera hearing and all evidence relating thereto shall be open to inspection only by the parties, the complainant, their attorneys and the court and its agents, and shall be used only as necessary for appellate review. At any probable cause hearing, the judge shall take cognizance of the evidence, if admissible, at the end of the in camera hearing without the questions being repeated or the evidence being resubmitted in open court. (1983, c. 701, s. 1.)

Rule 413. Medical actions; statements to ameliorate or mitigate adverse outcome.

Statements by a health care provider apologizing for an adverse outcome in medical treatment, offers to undertake corrective or remedial treatment or actions, and gratuitous acts to assist affected persons shall not be admissible to prove negligence or culpable conduct by the health care provider in an action brought under Article 1B of Chapter 90 of the General Statutes. (2004-149, s. 3.1.)

Rule 414. Evidence of medical expenses.

Evidence offered to prove past medical expenses shall be limited to evidence of the amounts actually paid to satisfy the bills that have been satisfied, regardless of the source of payment, and evidence of the amounts actually necessary to satisfy the bills that have been incurred but not yet satisfied. This rule does not impose upon any party an affirmative duty to seek a reduction in billed charges to which the party is not contractually entitled. (2011-283, s. 1.1; 2011-317, s. 1.1.)

Article 5.

Privileges.

Rule 501. General rule.

Except as otherwise required by the Constitution of the United States, the privileges of a witness, person, government, state, or political subdivision thereof shall be determined in accordance with the law of this State. (1983, c. 701, s. 1.)

Article 6.

Witnesses.

Rule 601. General rule of competency; disqualification of witness.

(a)   General rule. - Every person is competent to be a witness except as otherwise provided in these rules.

(b)   Disqualification of witness in general. - A person is disqualified to testify as a witness when the court determines that the person is (1) incapable of expressing himself or herself concerning the matter as to be understood, either directly or through interpretation by one who can understand him or her, or (2) incapable of understanding the duty of a witness to tell the truth.

(c)   Disqualification of interested persons. - Upon the trial of an action, or the hearing upon the merits of a special proceeding, a party or a person interested in the event, or a person from, through or under whom such a party or interested person derives his or her interest or title by assignment or otherwise, shall not be examined as a witness in his or her own behalf or interest, or in behalf of the party succeeding to his or her title or interest, against the executor, administrator or survivor of a deceased person, or the guardian of an incompetent person, or a person deriving his or her title or interest from, through or under a deceased or incompetent person by assignment or otherwise, concerning any oral communication between the witness and the deceased or incompetent person. However, this subdivision shall not apply when:

(1) The executor, administrator, survivor, guardian, or person so deriving title or interest is examined in his or her own behalf regarding the subject matter of the oral communication.

(2) The testimony of the deceased or incompetent person is given in evidence concerning the same transaction or communication.

(3) Evidence of the subject matter of the oral communication is offered by the executor, administrator, survivor, guardian or person so deriving title or interest.

Nothing in this subdivision shall preclude testimony as to the identity of the operator of a motor vehicle in any case. (1983, c. 701, s. 1; 2011-29, s. 2.)

Rule 602. Lack of personal knowledge.

A witness may not testify to a matter unless evidence is introduced sufficient to support a finding that he has personal knowledge of the matter. Evidence to prove personal knowledge may, but need not, consist of the testimony of the witness himself. This rule is subject to the provisions of Rule 703, relating to opinion testimony by expert witnesses. (1983, c. 701, s. 1.)

Rule 603. Oath or affirmation.

Before testifying, every witness shall be required to declare that he will testify truthfully, by oath or affirmation administered in a form calculated to awaken his conscience and impress his mind with his duty to do so. (1983, c. 701, s. 1.)

Rule 604. Interpreters.

An interpreter is subject to the provisions of these rules relating to qualification as an expert and the administration of an oath or affirmation that he will make a true translation. (1983, c. 701, s. 1.)

Rule 605. Competency of judge as witness.

The judge presiding at the trial may not testify in that trial as a witness. No objection need be made in order to preserve the point. (1983, c. 701, s. 1.)

Rule 606. Competency of juror as witness.

(a)   At the trial. - A member of the jury may not testify as a witness before that jury in the trial of the case in which he is sitting as a juror. If he is called so to testify, the opposing party shall be afforded an opportunity to object out of the presence of the jury.

(b)   Inquiry into validity of verdict or indictment. - Upon an inquiry into the validity of a verdict or indictment, a juror may not testify as to any matter or statement occurring during the course of the jury's deliberations or to the effect of anything upon his or any other juror's mind or emotions as influencing him to assent to or dissent from the verdict or indictment or concerning his mental processes in connection therewith, except that a juror may testify on the question whether extraneous prejudicial information was improperly brought to the jury's attention or whether any outside influence was improperly brought to bear upon any juror. Nor may his affidavit or evidence of any statement by him concerning a matter about which he would be precluded from testifying be received for these purposes. (1983, c. 701, s. 1.)

Rule 607. Who may impeach.

The credibility of a witness may be attacked by any party, including the party calling him. (1983, c. 701, s. 1.)

Rule 608. Evidence of character and conduct of witness.

(a) Opinion and reputation evidence of character. - The credibility of a witness may be attacked or supported by evidence in the form of reputation or opinion as provided in Rule 405(a), but subject to these limitations: (1) the evidence may refer only to character for truthfulness or untruthfulness, and (2) evidence of truthful character is admissible only after the character of the witness for truthfulness has been attacked by opinion or reputation evidence or otherwise.

(b) Specific instances of conduct. - Specific instances of the conduct of a witness, for the purpose of attacking or supporting his credibility, other than conviction of crime as provided in Rule 609, may not be proved by extrinsic evidence. They may, however, in the discretion of the court, if probative of truthfulness or untruthfulness, be inquired into on cross-examination of the witness (1) concerning his character for truthfulness or untruthfulness, or (2) concerning the character for truthfulness or untruthfulness of another witness as to which character the witness being cross-examined has testified.

The giving of testimony, whether by an accused or by any other witness, does not operate as a waiver of his privilege against self-incrimination when examined with respect to matters which relate only to credibility. (1983, c. 701, s. 1.)

Rule 609. Impeachment by evidence of conviction of crime.

(a) General rule. - For the purpose of attacking the credibility of a witness, evidence that the witness has been convicted of a felony, or of a Class A1, Class 1, or Class 2 misdemeanor, shall be admitted if elicited from the witness or established by public record during cross-examination or thereafter.

(b) Time limit. - Evidence of a conviction under this rule is not admissible if a period of more than 10 years has elapsed since the date of the conviction or of the release of the witness from the confinement imposed for that conviction, whichever is the later date, unless the court determines, in the interests of justice, that the probative value of the conviction supported by specific facts and circumstances substantially outweighs its prejudicial effect. However, evidence of a conviction more than 10 years old as calculated herein is not admissible unless the proponent gives to the adverse party sufficient advance written notice of intent to use such evidence to provide the adverse party with a fair opportunity to contest the use of such evidence.

(c) Effect of pardon. - Evidence of a conviction is not admissible under this rule if the conviction has been pardoned.

(d) Juvenile adjudications. - Evidence of juvenile adjudications is generally not admissible under this rule. The court may, however, in a criminal case allow evidence of a juvenile adjudication of a witness other than the accused if conviction of the offense would be admissible to attack the credibility of an adult and the court is satisfied that admission in evidence is necessary for a fair determination of the issue of guilt or innocence.

(e) Pendency of appeal. - The pendency of an appeal therefrom does not render evidence of a conviction inadmissible. Evidence of the pendency of an appeal is admissible. (1983, c. 701, s. 1; 1999-79, s. 1.)

Rule 610. Religious beliefs or opinions.

Evidence of the beliefs or opinions of a witness on matters of religion is not admissible for the purpose of showing that by reason of their nature his credibility is impaired or enhanced; provided, however, such evidence may be admitted for the purpose of showing interest or bias. (1983, c. 701, s. 1.)

Rule 611. Mode and order of interrogation and presentation.

(a) Control by court. - The court shall exercise reasonable control over the mode and order of interrogating witnesses and presenting evidence so as to (1) make the interrogation and presentation effective for the ascertainment of the truth, (2) avoid needless consumption of time, and (3) protect witnesses from harassment or undue embarrassment.

(b) Scope of cross-examination. - A witness may be cross-examined on any matter relevant to any issue in the case, including credibility.

(c) Leading questions. - Leading questions should not be used on the direct examination of a witness except as may be necessary to develop his testimony. Ordinarily leading questions should be permitted on cross-examination. When a party calls a hostile witness, an adverse party, or a witness identified with an adverse party, interrogation may be by leading questions. (1983, c. 701, s. 1.)

Rule 612. Writing or object used to refresh memory.

(a) While testifying. - If, while testifying, a witness uses a writing or object to refresh his memory, an adverse party is entitled to have the writing or object produced at the trial, hearing, or deposition in which the witness is testifying.

(b) Before testifying. - If, before testifying, a witness uses a writing or object to refresh his memory for the purpose of testifying and the court in its discretion determines that the interests of justice so require, an adverse party is entitled to have those portions of any writing or of the object which relate to the testimony produced, if practicable, at the trial, hearing, or deposition in which the witness is testifying.

(c) Terms and conditions of production and use. - A party entitled to have a writing or object produced under this rule is entitled to inspect it, to cross-examine the witness thereon, and to introduce in evidence those portions which relate to the testimony of the witness. If production of the writing or object at the trial, hearing, or deposition is impracticable, the court may order it made available for inspection. If it is claimed that the writing or object contains privileged information or information not directly related to the subject matter of the testimony, the court shall examine the writing or object in camera, excise any such portions, and order delivery of the remainder to the party entitled thereto. Any portion withheld over objections shall be preserved and made available to the appellate court in the event of an appeal. If a writing or object is not produced, made available for inspection, or delivered pursuant to order under this rule, the court shall make any order justice requires, but in criminal cases if the prosecution elects not to comply, the order shall be one striking the testimony or, if justice so requires, declaring a mistrial. (1983, c. 701, s. 1.)

Rule 613. Prior statements of witnesses.

In examining a witness concerning a prior statement made by him, whether written or not, the statement need not be shown nor its contents disclosed to him at that time, but on request the same shall be shown or disclosed to opposing counsel. (1983, c. 701, s. 1.)

Rule 614. Calling and interrogation of witnesses by court.

(a) Calling by court. - The court may, on its own motion or at the suggestion of a party, call witnesses, and all parties are entitled to cross-examine witnesses thus called.

(b) Interrogation by court. - The court may interrogate witnesses, whether called by itself or by a party.

(c) Objections. - No objections are necessary with respect to the calling of a witness by the court or to questions propounded to a witness by the court but it shall be deemed that proper objection has been made and overruled. (1983, c. 701, s. 1.)

Rule 615. Exclusion of witnesses.

At the request of a party the court may order witnesses excluded so that they cannot hear the testimony of other witnesses, and it may make the order of its own motion. This rule does not authorize exclusion of (1) a party who is a natural person, or (2) an officer or employee of a party that is not a natural person designated as its representative by its attorney, or (3) a person whose presence is shown by a party to be essential to the presentation of his cause, or (4) a person whose presence is determined by the court to be in the interest of justice. (1983, c. 701, s. 1.)

Rule 616. Alternative testimony of witnesses with developmental disabilities or mental retardation in civil cases and special proceedings.

(a) Definitions. - The following definitions apply to this section:

(1) The definitions set out in G.S. 122C-3.

(2) "Remote testimony" means a method by which a witness testifies outside of an open forum and outside of the physical presence of a party or parties.

(b) Remote Testimony Authorized. - A person with a developmental disability or a person with mental retardation who is competent to testify may testify by remote testimony in a civil proceeding or special proceeding if the court determines by clear and convincing evidence that the witness would suffer serious emotional distress from testifying in the presence of a named party or parties or from testifying in an open forum and that the ability of the witness to communicate with the trier of fact would be impaired by testifying in the presence of a named party or parties or from testifying in an open forum.

(c) Hearing Procedure. - Upon motion of a party or the court's own motion, and for good cause shown, the court shall hold an evidentiary hearing to determine whether to allow remote testimony. The hearing shall be recorded unless recordation is waived by all parties. The presence of the witness is not required at the hearing unless so ordered by the presiding judge.

(d) Order. - An order allowing or disallowing the use of remote testimony shall state the findings and conclusions of law that support the court's determination. An order allowing the use of remote testimony also shall do all of the following:

(1) State the method by which the witness is to testify.

(2) List any individual or category of individuals allowed to be in or required to be excluded from the presence of the witness during testimony.

(3) State any special conditions necessary to facilitate the cross-examination of the witness.

(4) State any condition or limitation upon the participation of individuals in the presence of the witness during the testimony.

(5) State any other conditions necessary for taking or presenting testimony.

(e) Testimony. - The method of remote testimony shall allow the trier of fact and all parties to observe the demeanor of the witness as the witness testifies in a similar manner as if the witness were testifying in the open forum. Except as provided in this section, the court shall ensure that the counsel for all parties is physically present where the witness testifies and has a full and fair opportunity for examination and cross-examination of the witness. In a proceeding where a party is representing itself, the court may limit or deny the party from being physically present during testimony if the court finds that the witness would suffer serious emotional distress from testifying in the presence of the party. A party may waive the right to have counsel physically present where the witness testifies.

(f) Nonexclusive Procedure and Standard. - Nothing in this section shall prohibit the use or application of any other method or procedure authorized or required by law for the introduction into evidence of statements or testimony of a person with a developmental disability or a person with mental retardation. (2009-514, s. 1.)

Article 7.

Opinions and Expert Testimony.

Rule 701. Opinion testimony by lay witness.

If the witness is not testifying as an expert, his testimony in the form of opinions or inferences is limited to those opinions or inferences which are (a) rationally based on the perception of the witness and (b) helpful to a clear understanding of his testimony or the determination of a fact in issue. (1983, c. 701, s. 1.)

Rule 702. Testimony by experts.

(a) If scientific, technical or other specialized knowledge will assist the trier of fact to understand the evidence or to determine a fact in issue, a witness qualified as an expert by knowledge, skill, experience, training, or education, may testify thereto in the form of an opinion, or otherwise, if all of the following apply:

(1) The testimony is based upon sufficient facts or data.

(2) The testimony is the product of reliable principles and methods.

(3) The witness has applied the principles and methods reliably to the facts of the case.

(a1) A witness, qualified under subsection (a) of this section and with proper foundation, may give expert testimony solely on the issue of impairment and not on the issue of specific alcohol concentration level relating to the following:

(1) The results of a Horizontal Gaze Nystagmus (HGN) Test when the test is administered by a person who has successfully completed training in HGN.

(2) Whether a person was under the influence of one or more impairing substances, and the category of such impairing substance or substances. A witness who has received training and holds a current certification as a Drug Recognition Expert, issued by the State Department of Health and Human Services, shall be qualified to give the testimony under this subdivision.

(b) In a medical malpractice action as defined in G.S. 90-21.11, a person shall not give expert testimony on the appropriate standard of health care as defined in G.S. 90-21.12 unless the person is a licensed health care provider in this State or another state and meets the following criteria:

(1) If the party against whom or on whose behalf the testimony is offered is a specialist, the expert witness must:

a. Specialize in the same specialty as the party against whom or on whose behalf the testimony is offered; or

b. Specialize in a similar specialty which includes within its specialty the performance of the procedure that is the subject of the complaint and have prior experience treating similar patients.

(2) During the year immediately preceding the date of the occurrence that is the basis for the action, the expert witness must have devoted a majority of his or her professional time to either or both of the following:

a. The active clinical practice of the same health profession in which the party against whom or on whose behalf the testimony is offered, and if that party is a specialist, the active clinical practice of the same specialty or a similar specialty which includes within its specialty the performance of the procedure that is the subject of the complaint and have prior experience treating similar patients; or

b. The instruction of students in an accredited health professional school or accredited residency or clinical research program in the same health profession in which the party against whom or on whose behalf the testimony is offered, and if that party is a specialist, an accredited health professional school or accredited residency or clinical research program in the same specialty.

(c) Notwithstanding subsection (b) of this section, if the party against whom or on whose behalf the testimony is offered is a general practitioner, the expert witness, during the year immediately preceding the date of the occurrence that is the basis for the action, must have devoted a majority of his or her professional time to either or both of the following:

(1) Active clinical practice as a general practitioner; or

(2) Instruction of students in an accredited health professional school or accredited residency or clinical research program in the general practice of medicine.

(d) Notwithstanding subsection (b) of this section, a physician who qualifies as an expert under subsection (a) of this Rule and who by reason of active clinical practice or instruction of students has knowledge of the applicable standard of care for nurses, nurse practitioners, certified registered nurse anesthetists, certified registered nurse midwives, physician assistants, or other medical support staff may give expert testimony in a medical malpractice action with respect to the standard of care of which he is knowledgeable of nurses, nurse practitioners, certified registered nurse anesthetists, certified registered nurse midwives, physician assistants licensed under Chapter 90 of the General Statutes, or other medical support staff.

(e) Upon motion by either party, a resident judge of the superior court in the county or judicial district in which the action is pending may allow expert testimony on the appropriate standard of health care by a witness who does not meet the requirements of subsection (b) or (c) of this Rule, but who is otherwise qualified as an expert witness, upon a showing by the movant of extraordinary circumstances and a determination by the court that the motion should be allowed to serve the ends of justice.

(f) In an action alleging medical malpractice, an expert witness shall not testify on a contingency fee basis.

(g) This section does not limit the power of the trial court to disqualify an expert witness on grounds other than the qualifications set forth in this section.

(h) Notwithstanding subsection (b) of this section, in a medical malpractice action as defined in G.S. 90-21.11(2)b. against a hospital, or other health care or medical facility, a person shall not give expert testimony on the appropriate standard of care as to administrative or other nonclinical issues unless the person has substantial knowledge, by virtue of his or her training and experience, about the standard of care among hospitals, or health care or medical facilities, of the same type as the hospital, or health care or medical facility, whose actions or inactions are the subject of the testimony situated in the same or similar communities at the time of the alleged act giving rise to the cause of action.

(i) A witness qualified as an expert in accident reconstruction who has performed a reconstruction of a crash, or has reviewed the report of investigation, with proper foundation may give an opinion as to the speed of a vehicle even if the witness did not observe the vehicle moving. (1983, c. 701, s. 1; 1995, c. 309, s. 1; 2006-253, s. 6; 2007-493, s. 5; 2011-283, s. 1.3; 2011-400, s. 4.)

Rule 703. Bases of opinion testimony by experts.

The facts or data in the particular case upon which an expert bases an opinion or inference may be those perceived by or made known to him at or before the hearing. If of a type reasonably relied upon by experts in the particular field in forming opinions or inferences upon the subject, the facts or data need not be admissible in evidence. (1983, c. 701, s. 1.)

Rule 704. Opinion on ultimate issue.

Testimony in the form of an opinion or inference is not objectionable because it embraces an ultimate issue to be decided by the trier of fact. (1983, c. 701, s. 1.)

Rule 705. Disclosure of facts or data underlying expert opinion.

The expert may testify in terms of opinion or inference and give his reasons therefor without prior disclosure of the underlying facts or data, unless an adverse party requests otherwise, in which event the expert will be required to disclose such underlying facts or data on direct examination or voir dire before stating the opinion. The expert may in any event be required to disclose the underlying facts or data on cross-examination. There shall be no requirement that expert testimony be in response to a hypothetical question. (1983, c. 701, s. 1.)

Rule 706. Court appointed experts.

(a) Appointment. - The court may on its own motion or on the motion of any party enter an order to show cause why expert witnesses should not be appointed, and may request the parties to submit nominations. The court may appoint any expert witnesses agreed upon by the parties, and may appoint witnesses of its own selection. An expert witness shall not be appointed by the court unless he consents to act. A witness so appointed shall be informed of his duties by the court in writing, a copy of which shall be filed with the clerk, or at a conference in which the parties shall have opportunity to participate. A witness so appointed shall advise the parties of his findings, if any; his deposition may be taken by any party; and he may be called to testify by the court or any party. He shall be subject to cross-examination by each party, including a party calling him as a witness.

(b) Compensation. - Expert witnesses so appointed are entitled to reasonable compensation in whatever sum the court may allow. The compensation thus fixed is payable from funds which may be provided by law in criminal cases and civil actions and proceedings involving just compensation for the taking of property. In other civil actions and proceedings the compensation shall be paid by the parties in such proportion and at such time as the court directs, and thereafter charged in like manner as other costs.

(c) Disclosure of appointment. - In the exercise of its discretion, the court may authorize disclosure to the jury of the fact that the court appointed the expert witness.

(d) Parties' experts of own selection. - Nothing in this rule limits the parties in calling expert witnesses of their own selection. (1983, c. 701, s. 1.)

Article 8.

Hearsay.

Rule 801. Definitions and exception for admissions of a party-opponent.

The following definitions apply under this Article:

(a) Statement. - A "statement" is (1) an oral or written assertion or (2) nonverbal conduct of a person, if it is intended by him as an assertion.

(b)   Declarant. - A "declarant" is a person who makes a statement.

(c)   Hearsay. - "Hearsay" is a statement, other than one made by the declarant while testifying at the trial or hearing, offered in evidence to prove the truth of the matter asserted.

(d)   Exception for Admissions by a Party-Opponent. - A statement is admissible as an exception to the hearsay rule if it is offered against a party and it is (A) his own statement, in either his individual or a representative capacity, or (B) a statement of which he has manifested his adoption or belief in its truth, or (C) a statement by a person authorized by him to make a statement concerning the subject, or (D) a statement by his agent or servant concerning a matter within the scope of his agency or employment, made during the existence of the relationship or (E) a statement by a coconspirator of such party during the course and in furtherance of the conspiracy. (1983, c. 701, s. 1.)

Rule 802. Hearsay rule.

Hearsay is not admissible except as provided by statute or by these rules. (1983, c. 701, s. 1.)

Rule 803. Hearsay exceptions; availability of declarant immaterial.

The following are not excluded by the hearsay rule, even though the declarant is available as a witness:

(1)   Present Sense Impression. - A statement describing or explaining an event or condition made while the declarant was perceiving the event or condition, or immediately thereafter.

(2)   Excited Utterance. - A statement relating to a startling event or condition made while the declarant was under the stress of excitement caused by the event or condition.

(3)   Then Existing Mental, Emotional, or Physical Condition. - A statement of the declarant's then existing state of mind, emotion, sensation, or physical condition (such as intent, plan, motive, design, mental feeling, pain, and bodily health), but not including a statement of memory or belief to prove the fact

remembered or believed unless it relates to the execution, revocation, identification, or terms of declarant's will.

(4) Statements for Purposes of Medical Diagnosis or Treatment. - Statements made for purposes of medical diagnosis or treatment and describing medical history, or past or present symptoms, pain, or sensations, or the inception or general character of the cause or external source thereof insofar as reasonably pertinent to diagnosis or treatment.

(5) Recorded Recollection. - A memorandum or record concerning a matter about which a witness once had knowledge but now has insufficient recollection to enable him to testify fully and accurately, shown to have been made or adopted by the witness when the matter was fresh in his memory and to reflect that knowledge correctly. If admitted, the memorandum or record may be read into evidence but may not itself be received as an exhibit unless offered by an adverse party.

(6) Records of Regularly Conducted Activity. - A memorandum, report, record, or data compilation, in any form, of acts, events, conditions, opinions, or diagnoses, made at or near the time by, or from information transmitted by, a person with knowledge, if kept in the course of a regularly conducted business activity, and if it was the regular practice of that business activity to make the memorandum, report, record, or data compilation, all as shown by the testimony of the custodian or other qualified witness, unless the source of information or the method or circumstances of preparation indicate lack of trustworthiness. The term "business" as used in this paragraph includes business, institution, association, profession, occupation, and calling of every kind, whether or not conducted for profit.

(7) Absence of Entry in Records Kept in Accordance with the Provisions of Paragraph (6). - Evidence that a matter is not included in the memoranda, reports, records, or data compilations, in any form, kept in accordance with the provisions of paragraph (6), to prove the nonoccurrence or nonexistence of the matter, if the matter was of a kind of which a memorandum, report, record, or data compilation was regularly made and preserved, unless the sources of information or other circumstances indicate lack of trustworthiness.

(8) Public Records and Reports. - Records, reports, statements, or data compilations, in any form, of public offices or agencies, setting forth (A) the activities of the office or agency, or (B) matters observed pursuant to duty imposed by law as to which matters there was a duty to report, excluding,

however, in criminal cases matters observed by police officers and other law-enforcement personnel, or (C) in civil actions and proceedings and against the State in criminal cases, factual findings resulting from an investigation made pursuant to authority granted by law, unless the sources of information or other circumstances indicate lack of trustworthiness.

(9)   Records of Vital Statistics. - Records or data compilations, in any form, of births, fetal deaths, deaths, or marriages, if the report thereof was made to a public office pursuant to requirements of law.

(10)   Absence of Public Record or Entry. - To prove the absence of a record, report, statement, or data compilation, in any form, or the nonoccurrence or nonexistence of a matter of which a record, report, statement, or data compilation, in any form, was regularly made and preserved by a public office or agency, evidence in the form of a certification in accordance with Rule 902, or testimony, that diligent search failed to disclose the record, report, statement, or data compilation, or entry.

(11)   Records of Religious Organizations. - Statements of births, marriages, divorces, deaths, legitimacy, ancestry, relationship by blood or marriage, or other similar facts of personal or family history, contained in a regularly kept record of a religious organization.

(12)   Marriage, Baptismal, and Similar Certificates. - Statements of fact contained in a certificate that the maker performed a marriage or other ceremony or administered a sacrament, made by a clergyman, public official, or other person authorized by the rules or practices of a religious organization or by law to perform the act certified, and purporting to have been issued at the time of the act or within a reasonable time thereafter.

(13)   Family Records. - Statements of fact concerning personal or family history contained in family Bibles, genealogies, charts, engravings on rings, inscriptions on family portraits, engravings on urns, crypts, or tombstones, or the like.

(14)   Records of Documents Affecting an Interest in Property. - The record of a document purporting to establish or affect an interest in property, as proof of the content of the original recorded document and its execution and delivery by each person by whom it purports to have been executed, if the record is a record of a public office and an applicable statute authorizes the recording of documents of that kind in that office.

(15) Statements in Documents Affecting an Interest in Property. - A statement contained in a document purporting to establish or affect an interest in property if the matter stated was relevant to the purpose of the document, unless dealings with the property since the document was made have been inconsistent with the truth of the statement or the purport of the document.

(16) Statements in Ancient Documents. - Statements in a document in existence 20 years or more the authenticity of which is established.

(17) Market Reports, Commercial Publications. - Market quotations, tabulations, lists, directories, or other published compilations, generally used and relied upon by the public or by persons in particular occupations.

(18) Learned Treatises. - To the extent called to the attention of an expert witness upon cross-examination or relied upon by him in direct examination, statements contained in published treatises, periodicals, or pamphlets on a subject of history, medicine, or other science or art, established as a reliable authority by the testimony or admission of the witness or by other expert testimony or by judicial notice. If admitted, the statements may be read into evidence but may not be received as exhibits.

(19) Reputation Concerning Personal or Family History. - Reputation among members of his family by blood, adoption, or marriage, or among his associates, or in the community, concerning a person's birth, adoption, marriage, divorce, death, legitimacy, relationship by blood, adoption, or marriage, ancestry, or other similar fact of his personal or family history.

(20) Reputation Concerning Boundaries or General History. - Reputation in a community, arising before the controversy, as to boundaries of or customs affecting lands in the community, and reputation as to events of general history important to the community or state or nation in which located.

(21) Reputation as to Character. - Reputation of a person's character among his associates or in the community.

(22) (Reserved).

(23) Judgment as to Personal, Family or General History, or Boundaries. - Judgments as proof of matters of personal, family or general history, or

boundaries, essential to the judgment, if the same would be provable by evidence of reputation.

(24) Other Exceptions. - A statement not specifically covered by any of the foregoing exceptions but having equivalent circumstantial guarantees of trustworthiness, if the court determines that (A) the statement is offered as evidence of a material fact; (B) the statement is more probative on the point for which it is offered than any other evidence which the proponent can procure through reasonable efforts; and (C) the general purposes of these rules and the interests of justice will best be served by admission of the statement into evidence. However, a statement may not be admitted under this exception unless the proponent of it gives written notice stating his intention to offer the statement and the particulars of it, including the name and address of the declarant, to the adverse party sufficiently in advance of offering the statement to provide the adverse party with a fair opportunity to prepare to meet the statement. (1983, c. 701, s. 1.)

Rule 804. Hearsay exceptions; declarant unavailable.

(a) Definition of unavailability. - "Unavailability as a witness" includes situations in which the declarant:

(1) Is exempted by ruling of the court on the ground of privilege from testifying concerning the subject matter of his statement; or

(2) Persists in refusing to testify concerning the subject matter of his statement despite an order of the court to do so; or

(3) Testifies to a lack of memory of the subject matter of his statement; or

(4) Is unable to be present or to testify at the hearing because of death or then existing physical or mental illness or infirmity; or

(5) Is absent from the hearing and the proponent of his statement has been unable to procure his attendance (or in the case of a hearsay exception under subdivision (b)(2), (3), or (4), his attendance or testimony) by process or other reasonable means.

A declarant is not unavailable as a witness if his exemption, refusal, claim of lack of memory, inability, or absence is due to the procurement or wrongdoing of the proponent of his statement for the purpose of preventing the witness from attending or testifying.

(b)   Hearsay exceptions. - The following are not excluded by the hearsay rule if the declarant is unavailable as a witness:

(1)   Former Testimony. - Testimony given as a witness at another hearing of the same or a different proceeding, or in a deposition taken in compliance with law in the course of the same or another proceeding, if the party against whom the testimony is now offered, or, in a civil action or proceeding, a predecessor in interest, had an opportunity and similar motive to develop the testimony by direct, cross, or redirect examination.

(2)   Statement Under Belief of Impending Death. - A statement made by a declarant while believing that his death was imminent, concerning the cause or circumstances of what he believed to be his impending death.

(3)   Statement Against Interest. - A statement which was at the time of its making so far contrary to the declarant's pecuniary or proprietary interest, or so far tended to subject him to civil or criminal liability, or to render invalid a claim by him against another, that a reasonable man in his position would not have made the statement unless he believed it to be true. A statement tending to expose the declarant to criminal liability is not admissible in a criminal case unless corroborating circumstances clearly indicate the trustworthiness of the statement.

(4)   Statement of Personal or Family History. - (A) A statement concerning the declarant's own birth, adoption, marriage, divorce, legitimacy, relationship by blood, adoption, or marriage, ancestry, or other similar fact of personal or family history, even though declarant had no means of acquiring personal knowledge of the matter stated; or (B) a statement concerning the foregoing matters, and death also, of another person, if the declarant was related to the other by blood, adoption, or marriage or was so intimately associated with the other's family as to be likely to have accurate information concerning the matter declared.

(5)   Other Exceptions. - A statement not specifically covered by any of the foregoing exceptions but having equivalent circumstantial guarantees of trustworthiness, if the court determines that (A) the statement is offered as evidence of a material fact; (B) the statement is more probative on the point for which it is offered than any other evidence which the proponent can procure through reasonable efforts; and (C) the general purposes of these rules and the

interests of justice will best be served by admission of the statement into evidence. However, a statement may not be admitted under this exception unless the proponent of it gives written notice stating his intention to offer the statement and the particulars of it, including the name and address of the declarant, to the adverse party sufficiently in advance of offering the statement to provide the adverse party with a fair opportunity to prepare to meet the statement. (1983, c. 701, s. 1.)

Rule 805. Hearsay within hearsay.

Hearsay included within hearsay is not excluded under the hearsay rule if each part of the combined statements conforms with an exception to the hearsay rule provided in these rules. (1983, c. 701, s. 1.)

Rule 806. Attacking and supporting credibility of declarant.

When a hearsay statement has been admitted in evidence, the credibility of the declarant may be attacked, and if attacked may be supported, by any evidence which would be admissible for those purposes if declarant had testified as a witness. Evidence of a statement or conduct by the declarant at any time, inconsistent with his hearsay statement, is not subject to any requirement that he may have been afforded an opportunity to deny or explain. If the party against whom a hearsay statement has been admitted calls the declarant as a witness, the party is entitled to examine him on the statement as if under cross-examination. (1983, c. 701, s. 1.)

Article 9.

Authentication and Identification.

Rule 901. Requirement of authentication or identification.

(a)   General provision. - The requirement of authentication or identification as a condition precedent to admissibility is satisfied by evidence sufficient to support a finding that the matter in question is what its proponent claims.

(b)   Illustrations. - By way of illustration only, and not by way of limitation, the following are examples of authentication or identification conforming with the requirements of this rule:

(1) Testimony of Witness with Knowledge. - Testimony that a matter is what it is claimed to be.

(2) Nonexpert Opinion on Handwriting. - Nonexpert opinion as to the genuineness of handwriting, based upon familiarity not acquired for purposes of the litigation.

(3) Comparison by Trier or Expert Witness. - Comparison by the trier of fact or by expert witnesses with specimens which have been authenticated.

(4) Distinctive Characteristics and the Like. - Appearance, contents, substance, internal patterns, or other distinctive characteristics, taken in conjunction with circumstances.

(5) Voice Identification. - Identification of a voice, whether heard firsthand or through mechanical or electronic transmission or recording, by opinion based upon hearing the voice at any time under circumstances connecting it with the alleged speaker.

(6) Telephone Conversations. - Telephone conversations, by evidence that a call was made to the number assigned at the time by the telephone company to a particular person or business, if (A) in the case of a person, circumstances, including self-identification, show the person answering to be the one called, or (B) in the case of a business, the call was made to a place of business and the conversation related to business reasonably transacted over the telephone.

(7) Public Records or Reports. - Evidence that a writing authorized by law to be recorded or filed and in fact recorded or filed in a public office, or a purported public record, report, statement, or data compilation, in any form, is from the public office where items of this nature are kept.

(8) Ancient Documents or Data Compilations. - Evidence that a document or data compilation, in any form, (A) is in such condition as to create no suspicion concerning its authenticity, (B) was in a place where it, if authentic, would likely be, and (C) has been in existence 20 years or more at the time it is offered.

(9) Process or System. - Evidence describing a process or system used to produce a result and showing that the process or system produces an accurate result.

(10) Methods Provided by Statute. - Any method of authentication or identification provided by statute. (1983, c. 701, s. 1.)

Rule 902. Self-authentication.

Extrinsic evidence of authenticity as a condition precedent to admissibility is not required with respect to the following:

(1) Domestic Public Documents Under Seal. - A document bearing a seal purporting to be that of the United States, or of any state, district, commonwealth, territory or insular possession thereof, or the Trust Territory of the Pacific Islands, or of a political subdivision, department, officer, or agency thereof, and a signature purporting to be an attestation or execution.

(2) Domestic Public Documents Not Under Seal. - A document purporting to bear the signature in his official capacity of an officer or employee of any entity included in paragraph (1) hereof, having no seal, if a public officer having a seal and having official duties in the district or political subdivision of the officer or employee certifies under seal that the signer has the official capacity and that the signature is genuine.

(3) Foreign Public Documents. - A document purporting to be executed or attested in his official capacity by a person authorized by the laws of a foreign country to make the execution or attestation, and accompanied by a final certification as to the genuineness of the signature and official position (A) of the executing or attesting person, or (B) of any foreign official whose certificate of genuineness of signature and official position relates to the execution or attestation or is in a chain of certificates of genuineness of signature and official position relating to the execution or attestation. A final certification may be made by a secretary of embassy or legation, consul general, consul, vice consul, or consular agent of the United States, or a diplomatic or consular official of the foreign country assigned or accredited to the United States. If reasonable opportunity has been given to all parties to investigate the authenticity and accuracy of official documents, the court may, for good cause shown, order that they be treated as presumptively authentic without final certification or permit them to be evidenced by an attested summary with or without final certification.

(4) Certified Copies of Public Records. - A copy of an official record or report or entry therein, or of a document authorized by law to be recorded or filed and actually recorded or filed in a public office, including data compilations

in any form, certified as correct by the custodian or other person authorized to make the certification, by certificate complying with paragraph (1), (2), or (3) or complying with any law of the United States or of this State.

(5) Official Publications. - Books, pamphlets, or other publications purporting to be issued by public authority.

(6) Newspapers and Periodicals. - Printed materials purporting to be newspapers or periodicals.

(7) Trade Inscriptions and the Like. - Inscriptions, signs, tags, or labels purporting to have been affixed in the course of business and indicating ownership, control, or origin.

(8) Acknowledged Documents. - Documents accompanied by a certificate of acknowledgment executed in the manner provided by law by a notary public or other officer authorized by law to take acknowledgments.

(9) Commercial Paper and Related Documents. - Commercial paper, signatures thereon, and documents relating thereto to the extent provided by general commercial law.

(10) Presumptions Created by Law. - Any signature, document, or other matter declared by any law of the United States or of this State to be presumptively or prima facie genuine or authentic. (1983, c. 701, s. 1.)

Rule 903. Subscribing witness' testimony unnecessary.

The testimony of a subscribing witness is not necessary to authenticate a writing unless required by the laws of the jurisdiction whose laws govern the validity of the writing. (1983, c. 701, s. 1.)

Article 10.

Contents of Writings, Recordings and Photographs.

Rule 1001. Definitions.

For the purposes of this Article the following definitions are applicable:

(1) Writings and Recordings. - "Writings" and "recordings" consist of letters, words, sounds, or numbers, or their equivalent, set down by handwriting, typewriting, printing, photostating, photographing, magnetic impulse, mechanical or electronic recording, or other form of data compilation.

(2) Photographs. - "Photographs" include still photographs, x-ray films, video tapes, and motion pictures.

(3) Original. - An "original" of a writing or recording is the writing or recording itself or any counterpart intended to have the same effect by a person executing or issuing it. An "original" of a photograph includes the negative or any print therefrom. If data are stored in a computer or similar device, any printout or other output readable by sight, shown to reflect the data accurately, is an "original."

(4) Duplicate. - A "duplicate" is a counterpart produced by the same impression as the original, or from the same matrix, or by means of photography, including enlargements and miniatures, or by mechanical or electronic re-recording, or by chemical reproduction, or by other equivalent techniques which accurately reproduce the original. (1983, c. 701, s. 1.)

Rule 1002. Requirement of original.

To prove the content of a writing, recording, or photograph, the original writing, recording, or photograph is required, except as otherwise provided in these rules or by statute. (1983, c. 701, s. 1.)

Rule 1003. Admissibility of duplicates.

A duplicate is admissible to the same extent as an original unless (1) a genuine question is raised as to the authenticity of the original or (2) in the circumstances it would be unfair to admit the duplicate in lieu of the original. (1983, c. 701, s. 1.)

Rule 1004. Admissibility of other evidence of contents.

The original is not required, and other evidence of the contents of a writing, recording, or photograph is admissible if:

(1) Originals Lost or Destroyed. - All originals are lost or have been destroyed, unless the proponent lost or destroyed them in bad faith; or

(2) Original Not Obtainable. - No original can be obtained by any available judicial process or procedure; or

(3) Original in Possession of Opponent. - At a time when an original was under the control of a party against whom offered, he was put on notice, by the pleadings or otherwise, that the contents would be a subject of proof at the hearing, and he does not produce the original at the hearing; or

(4) Collateral Matters. - The writing, recording, or photograph is not closely related to a controlling issue. (1983, c. 701, s. 1.)

Rule 1005. Public records.

The contents of an official record, or of a document authorized to be recorded or filed and actually recorded or filed, including data compilations in any form, if otherwise admissible, may be proved by copy, certified as correct in accordance with Rule 902 or testified to be correct by a witness who has compared it with the original. If a copy which complies with the foregoing cannot be obtained by the exercise of reasonable diligence, then other evidence of the contents may be given. (1983, c. 701, s. 1.)

Rule 1006. Summaries.

The contents of voluminous writings, recordings, or photographs which cannot conveniently be examined in court may be presented in the form of a chart, summary, or calculation. The originals, or duplicates, shall be made available for examination or copying, or both, by other parties at a reasonable time and place. The court may order that they be produced in court. (1983, c. 701, s. 1.)

Rule 1007. Testimony or written admission of party.

Contents of writings, recordings, or photographs may be proved by the testimony or deposition of the party against whom offered or by his written admission, without accounting for the nonproduction of the original. (1983, c. 701, s. 1.)

Rule 1008. Functions of court and jury.

When the admissibility of other evidence of contents of writings, recordings, or photographs under these rules depends upon the fulfillment of a condition of fact, the question whether the condition has been fulfilled is ordinarily for the court to determine in accordance with the provisions of Rule 104. However, when an issue is raised (a) whether the asserted writing ever existed, or (b) whether another writing, recording, or photograph produced at the trial is the original, or (c) whether other evidence of contents correctly reflects the contents, the issue is for the trier of fact to determine as in the case of other issues of fact. (1983, c. 701, s. 1.)

Article 11.

Miscellaneous Rules.

Rule 1101. Applicability of rules.

(a) Proceedings generally. - Except as otherwise provided in subdivision (b) or by statute, these rules apply to all actions and proceedings in the courts of this State.

(b) Rules inapplicable. - The rules other than those with respect to privileges do not apply in the following situations:

(1) Preliminary Questions of Fact. - The determination of questions of fact preliminary to admissibility of evidence when the issue is to be determined by the court under Rule 104(a).

(2) Grand Jury. - Proceedings before grand juries.

(3) Miscellaneous Proceedings. - Proceedings for extradition or rendition; first appearance before district court judge or probable cause hearing in criminal cases; sentencing, or granting or revoking probation; issuance of warrants for arrest, criminal summonses, and search warrants; proceedings with respect to release on bail or otherwise.

(4) Contempt Proceedings. - Contempt proceedings in which the court is authorized by law to act summarily. (1983, c. 701, s. 1; 1983 (Reg. Sess., 1984), c. 1037, s. 14; 1985, c. 509, s. 2.)

Rule 1102. Short title.

These rules shall be known and may be cited as the "North Carolina Rules of Evidence." (1983, c. 701, s. 1.)

Article 1.

Jury Commissions, Preparation of Jury Lists, and Drawing of Panels.

§ 9-1. Jury commission in each county; membership; selection; oath; terms; expenses of jury system.

Not later than July 1, 1967, there shall be appointed in each county a jury commission of three members. One member of the commission shall be appointed by the senior regular resident superior court judge, one member by the clerk of superior court, and one member by the board of county commissioners. The appointees shall be qualified voters of the county, and shall serve for terms of two years. Appointees may be reappointed to successive terms. A vacancy in the commission shall be filled in the same manner as the original appointment, for the unexpired term. Each commissioner shall take an oath or affirmation that, without favor or prejudice, he will honestly perform the duties of a member of the jury commission during his term of service. The compensation of commissioners shall be fixed by the board of county commissioners, and shall be paid from the general fund of the county. All expenses necessary to carry out the provisions of this Chapter and to administer the jury system, including all data processing, document processing, supplies, postage, and other similar expenses, except as otherwise provided in this Chapter, shall be paid from the general fund of the county, except that the clerk of superior court shall furnish clerical or other personnel assistance, as the commission may reasonably require. (1967, c. 218, s. 1; 1981, c. 720, s. 3; 1991, c. 729, s. 1.)

§ 9-2. Preparation of master jury list; sources of names.

(a) It shall be the duty of the jury commission during every odd-numbered year to prepare a master list of prospective jurors qualified under this Chapter to serve in the biennium beginning on January 1 of the next year. Instead of providing a master list for an entire biennium, the commission may prepare a master list each year if the senior regular resident superior court judge requests in writing that it do so.

(b)　In preparing the master list, the jury commission shall use the list of registered voters and persons with drivers license records supplied to the county by the Commissioner of Motor Vehicles pursuant to G.S. 20-43.4. The commission may use fewer than all the names from the list if it uses a random method of selection. The commission may use other sources of names deemed by it to be reliable.

(c),　(d) Repealed by Session Laws 2003-226, s. 7(d), effective January 1, 2004.

(e)　The jury commission shall merge the entire list of names of each source used and randomly select the desired number of names to form the master list.

(f)　The master list shall contain not less than one and one-quarter times and not more than three times as many names as were drawn for jury duty in all courts in the county during the previous biennium, or, if an annual list is being prepared as requested under subsection (a) of this section the master list shall contain not less than one and one-quarter times and not more than three times as many names as were drawn for jury duty in all courts in the county during the previous year but in no event shall the list include fewer than 500 names, except that in counties in which a different panel of jurors is selected for each day of the week, there is no limit to the number of names that may be placed on the master list.

(g)　Repealed by Session Laws 2003-226, s. 7(d), effective January 1, 2004.

(h)　As used in this section "random" or "randomly" refers to a method of selection that results in each name on a list having an equal opportunity to be selected.

(i)　To facilitate random selection of jurors, all the names on the master list may be sorted into random order before the first panel is drawn. Thereafter, names may be selected sequentially from the randomized list without further randomization, except as required by G.S. 15A-1214.

(j)　The procedure for performing the preparation of the master list shall be in writing, adopted by the jury commission, and kept available for public inspection in the office of the clerk of court. The procedure must effectively preserve the authorized grounds for disqualification, the right of public access to the master list of prospective jurors as provided by G.S. 9-4, and the time sequence for drawing and summoning a jury panel.

(k)   In counties utilizing electronic data processing equipment, the functions of preparing and maintaining custody of the master list of prospective jurors, the procedure for drawing and summoning panels of jurors, and the procedure for maintaining records of names of jurors who have served, been excused or disqualified, or whose service has been deferred may be performed by this equipment, except that decisions as to mental or physical competence of prospective jurors shall continue to be made by jury commissioners. (1806, c. 694, P.R.; Code, ss. 1722, 1723; 1889, c. 559; 1897, cc. 117, 539; 1899, c. 729; Rev., s. 1957; C.S., s. 2312; 1947, c. 1007, s. 1; 1967, c. 218, s. 1; 1969, c. 205, s. 1; c. 1190, s. 49½; 1973, c. 83, ss. 1, 2; 1981, c. 430, s. 1; c. 720, s. 1; 1981 (Reg. Sess., 1982), c. 1226, s. 1; 1983, c. 197, s. 2; 2003-226, s. 7(d); 2007-512, s. 1; 2012-180, s. 1.)

§ 9-2.1: Repealed by Session Laws 2012-180, s. 2, effective July 12, 2012.

§ 9-3. Qualifications of prospective jurors.

All persons are qualified to serve as jurors and to be included on the master jury list who are citizens of the State and residents of the county, who have not served as jurors during the preceding two years or who have not served a full term of service as grand jurors during the preceding six years, who are 18 years of age or over, who are physically and mentally competent, who can understand the English language, who have not been convicted of a felony or pleaded guilty or nolo contendere to an indictment charging a felony (or if convicted of a felony or having pleaded guilty or nolo contendere to an indictment charging a felony have had their citizenship restored pursuant to law), and who have not been adjudged non compos mentis. Persons not qualified under this section are subject to challenge for cause. (1806, c. 694, P.R.; Code, ss. 1722, 1723; 1889, c. 559; 1897, cc. 117, 539; 1899, c. 729; Rev., s. 1957; C.S., s. 2312; 1947, c. 1007, s. 1; 1967, c. 218, s. 1; 1971, c. 1231, s. 1; 1973, c. 230, ss. 1, 2; 1977, c. 711, s. 10; 2011-42, s. 1; 2012-180, s. 3; 2013-148, s. 1.)

§ 9-4. Preparation and custody of alphabetized list; access to list.

(a) As the master jury list is prepared, the name of each qualified person selected for the list shall be recorded and alphabetically arranged. The alphabetized list shall be maintained in the office of the clerk of court, together with a statement of the sources used and procedures followed in preparing the list. The alphabetized list shall be kept under lock and key, but shall be available for public inspection during regular office hours. The clerk of court may elect to store an electronic copy of the alphabetized list for the county.

(b) Public access to juror information shall be limited to the alphabetized list of the names. The addresses and dates of birth of prospective jurors are confidential and not subject to disclosure without an order of the court. (1967, c. 218, s. 1; 1969, c. 205, s. 2; 2009-518, s. 1; 2012-18, s. 1.1; 2012-180, s. 4; 2013-166, s. 2.)

§ 9-5. Procedure for drawing panel of jurors.

At least 30 days prior to any session or sessions of superior or district court requiring a jury, the clerk of superior court or assistant or deputy clerk shall prepare or have electronically prepared a randomized list of names from the master jury list equal to the number of jurors required for the session or sessions scheduled. The clerk of superior court may decrease the number of randomized names to account for the addition of names of previously selected jurors whose service has been deferred to this session. For each week of a superior court session, the senior resident superior court judge for the district or set of districts as defined in G.S. 7A-41.1(a) in which the county is located shall specify the number of jurors to be drawn. For each week of a district court jury session, the chief district judge of the district court district in which the county is located shall specify the number of jurors to be drawn. Pooling of jurors between or among concurrent sessions of various courts is authorized in the discretion of the senior regular resident superior court judge. When pooling is utilized, the senior regular resident superior court judge, after consultation with the chief district judge when a district court jury is required, shall specify the total number of jurors to be drawn for such concurrent sessions. When grand jurors are needed, at least nine additional names shall be drawn.

The clerk of superior court shall either (i) prepare and issue the summonses or (ii) deliver the printed summonses or the list of names and addresses of jurors to the sheriff, who shall issue the summonses in accordance with the provisions of G.S. 9-10(a). The persons so summoned may serve as jurors in either the superior or the district court, or both, for the week for which summoned. Jurors who serve each week shall be discharged at the close of the weekly session or sessions, unless actually engaged in the trial of a case, and then they shall not be discharged until their service in that case is completed. (1806, c. 694, P.R.; 1868-9, c. 9, ss. 5, 6; c. 175; Code, ss. 1726, 1727, 1731; 1889, c. 559; 1897, c. 117; 1901, c. 28, s. 3; c. 636; 1903, c. 11; 1905, c. 38; c. 76, s. 4; c. 285; Rev., ss. 1958, 1959; C.S., ss. 2313, 2314; 1967, c. 218, s. 1; 1969, c. 205, s. 3; 1987 (Reg. Sess., 1988), c. 1037, s. 38; 2012-180, s. 5.)

§ 9-6. Jury service a public duty; excuses to be allowed in exceptional cases; procedure.

(a) The General Assembly hereby declares the public policy of this State to be that jury service is the solemn obligation of all qualified citizens, and that excuses from the discharge of this responsibility should be granted only for reasons of compelling personal hardship or because requiring service would be contrary to the public welfare, health, or safety.

(b) Pursuant to the foregoing policy, each chief district court judge shall promulgate procedures whereby he or any district court judge of his district court district designated by him, prior to the date that a jury session (or sessions) of superior or district court convenes, shall receive, hear, and pass on applications for excuses from jury duty. The procedures shall provide for the time and place, publicly announced, at which applications for excuses will be heard, and prospective jurors who have been summoned for service shall be so informed. In counties located in a district or set of districts as defined in G.S. 7A-41.1(a) which have a trial court administrator, the chief district judge may assign the duty of passing on applications for excuses from jury service to the administrator. In all cases concerning excuses, the clerk of court or the trial court administrator shall notify prospective jurors of the disposition of their excuses.

(c) A prospective juror excused by a judge in the exercise of the discretion conferred by subsection (b) may be required by the judge to serve as a juror in a subsequent session of court. If required to serve subsequently, the juror shall be considered on such occasion the same as if he were a member of the panel regularly summoned for jury service at that time.

(d) A judge hearing applications for excuses from jury duty shall excuse any person disqualified under § 9-3.

(e) The judge shall inform the clerk of superior court of persons excused under this section, and the clerk shall keep a record of excuses separate from the master jury list.

(f) The discretionary authority of a presiding judge to excuse a juror at the beginning of or during a session of court is not affected by this section. (1967, c. 218, s. 1; 1969, c. 205, ss. 4, 5; 1971, c. 377, s. 30; 1979, 2nd Sess., c. 1207, s. 1; 1981, c. 430, s. 2; 1985, c. 609, s. 2; 1987 (Reg. Sess., 1988), c. 1037, s. 47; 2012-180, s. 6.)

§ 9-6.1. Requests to be excused.

(a) Any person summoned as a juror who is 72 years or older and who wishes to be excused, deferred, or exempted may make the request without appearing in person by filing a signed statement of the ground of the request with the chief district court judge of that district, or the district court judge or trial court administrator designated by the chief district court judge pursuant to G.S. 9-6(b), at any time five business days before the date upon which the person is summoned to appear.

(b) Any person summoned as a juror who has a disability that could interfere with the person's ability to serve as a juror and who wishes to be excused, deferred, or exempted may make the request without appearing in person by filing a signed statement of the ground of the request, including a brief explanation of the disability that interferes with the person's ability to serve as a juror, with the chief district court judge of that district, or the district court judge or trial court administrator designated by the chief district court judge pursuant to G.S. 9-6(b), at any time five business days before the date upon which the person is summoned to appear. Upon request of the court, medical documentation of any disability may be submitted. Any privileged medical information or protected health information described in this section shall be confidential and shall be exempt from the provisions of Chapter 132 of the General Statutes or any other provision requiring information and records held by State agencies to be made public or accessible to the public.

(c) A person may request either a temporary or permanent exemption under this section, and the judge or trial court administrator may accept or reject either in the exercise of discretion conferred by G.S. 9-6(b), including the substitution of a temporary exemption for a requested permanent exemption. In the case of supplemental jurors summoned under G.S. 9-11, notice may be given when summoned. In case the chief district court judge, or the judge or trial court administrator designated by the chief district court judge pursuant to G.S. 9-6(b), rejects the request for exemption, the prospective juror shall be immediately notified by the trial court administrator or the clerk of court by telephone, letter, or personally. (1979, 2nd Sess., c. 1207, s. 2; 1981, c. 9, ss. 1, 2; c. 430, ss. 4, 5; 2005-149, s. 1; 2011-42, s. 2; 2012-180, s. 7.)

§ 9-7. Notation on master jury list of names of jurors who have served; retention.

(a) The names of persons summoned for jury service and the date or dates on which each person served shall be noted on the master jury list. This information shall be retained for two years, and persons shall be exempt from jury service for a period of two years from the date on which they were discharged from their prior service, except as provided in subsection (b) of this section.

(b) The names of persons summoned for jury service who served a full term on the grand jury pursuant to G.S. 15A-622, the date or dates on which each person served, and a notation that the person served the full term of service as a grand juror shall be noted on the master list. This information shall be retained for six years, and persons shall be exempt from jury service for a period of six years from the date on which they were discharged from their prior service. (1967, c. 218, s. 1; 2012-180, s. 8; 2013-148, s. 2.)

§ 9-7.1. Trial court administrator may assist clerk with performance of duties.

Upon the request of the clerk of superior court and with the agreement of the clerk of superior court and the senior resident superior court judge, the duties and responsibilities of the clerk of superior court under this Article may be assigned to the trial court administrator pursuant to G.S. 7A-356. (2012-180, s. 10.)

§§ 9-8 through 9-9. Repealed by Session Laws 1967, c. 218, s. 1.

Article 2.

Petit Jurors.

§ 9-10. Summons to jurors.

(a) The clerk of court shall serve the summons by first-class mail, or shall deliver either printed summonses or the list of the panel of prospective jurors to the sheriff of the county, who shall summon the persons named therein. The summons shall be served personally, or by leaving a copy thereof at the place of residence of the juror, or by telephone or first-class mail, at least 15 days before the session of court for which the juror is summoned. Service by telephone, or by first-class mail if mailed to the correct current address of the juror on or before the fifteenth day before the day the court convenes, shall be valid and binding on the person served, and he shall be bound to appear in the same manner as if personally served. The summons shall contain information as to the time, place, and authority before whom applications for excuses from jury service may be heard.

(b) All summons served personally or by mail under this section or under G.S. 9-11 shall inform the prospective juror that persons 72 years of age or older are entitled to establish in writing exemption from jury service for good cause, shall contain a statement for claiming such exemption and stating the cause and a place for the prospective juror's signature, and shall state the mailing address of the clerk of superior court and the date by which such request for exemption must be received. (1779, c. 157, ss. 4, 6, P.R.; R.C., c. 31, s. 29; 1868-9, c. 9, s. 12; Code, s. 1733; Rev., s. 1976; C.S., s. 2320; 1967, c. 218, s. 1; 1979, 2nd Sess., c. 1207, s. 3; 1985, c. 609, s. 3; 2006-226, s. 8; 2006-264, ss. 30(a), 30(c); 2012-180, s. 9.)

§ 9-11. Supplemental jurors; special venire.

(a) If necessary, the court may, without using the jury list, order the sheriff to summon from day to day additional jurors to supplement the original venire. Jurors so summoned shall have the same qualifications and be subject to the same challenges as jurors selected for the regular jury list. If the presiding judge finds that service of summons by the sheriff is not suitable because of his direct or indirect interest in the action to be tried, the judge may appoint some suitable person in place of the sheriff to summon supplemental jurors. The clerk of superior court shall keep a record of the names of those additional jurors who are so summoned and who report for jury service.

(b) The presiding judge may, in his discretion, at any time before or during a session direct that supplemental jurors or a special venire be selected from the jury list in the same manner as is provided for the selection of regular jurors. Jurors summoned under this subsection may be discharged by the court at any time during the session and are subject to the same challenges as regular jurors, and to no other challenges. (1779, c. 156, s. 69, P.R.; 1830, c. 27; R.C., c. 31, s. 29; c. 35, ss. 30, 31; Code, ss. 1733, 1738, 1739, 1740; 1887, c. 53; 1889, c. 441; 1897, c. 364; Rev., ss. 1967, 1968, 1973, 1974, 1975, 3265, 3602; 1911, c. 15; 1913, c. 31, ss. 1, 2; 1915, c. 210; C.S., ss. 2321, 2322, 2338, 2339, 2340, 4635; 1967, c. 218, s. 1; 1969, c. 205, s. 6; 2012-180, s. 11.)

§ 9-12. Supplemental jurors from other counties.

(a) On motion of any party or the State, or on his own motion, any judge of the superior court, if he is of the opinion that it is necessary in order to provide a fair trial in any case, and regardless of whether he will preside over the trial of that case, may order as many jurors as he deems necessary to be summoned from any county or counties in the district or set of districts as defined in G.S. 7A-41.1(a) in which the county of trial is located or in any adjoining district or set of districts. These jurors shall be selected and shall serve in the manner provided for selection and service of supplemental jurors selected from the jury list. These jurors shall be subject to the same challenges as other jurors, except challenges for nonresidence in the county of trial.

(b) Transportation may be furnished in lieu of mileage.

(c) Repealed by Session Laws 1971, c. 377, s. 32. (1913, c. 4, ss. 1, 2; C.S., s. 473; 1931, c. 308; 1933, c. 248; 1961, c. 110; 1967, c. 218, s. 1; 1971, c. 377, s. 32; 1987 (Reg. Sess., 1988), c. 1037, s. 48.)

§ 9-13. Penalty for disobeying summons.

Every person summoned to appear as a juror who has not been excused, and who fails to appear and attend until duly discharged, shall be subject to a fine of not more than fifty dollars ($50.00), to be imposed by the court, unless he renders an excuse deemed sufficient. The forfeiture so imposed if not paid forthwith shall be entered as a judgment against the defaulting juror, and the clerk of superior court shall issue an execution against his estate. (1779, c. 157, s. 4, P.R.; 1783, c. 189, P.R.; 1806, c. 694, P.R.; R.C., c. 31, s. 30; Code, ss. 405, 1734; Rev., s. 1977; C.S., s. 2323; 1967, c. 218, s. 1.)

§ 9-14. Jury sworn; judge decides competency.

The clerk shall, at the beginning of court, swear all jurors who have not been selected as grand jurors. Each juror shall take (i) the oath required by Section 7 of Article VI of the Constitution of North Carolina, by swearing or affirming to support and maintain the Constitution of the United States and the Constitution and laws of North Carolina not inconsistent therewith and (ii) the oath required under G.S. 11-11, by swearing or affirming to truthfully and without prejudice or partiality try all issues in criminal or civil actions that come before the juror and give true verdicts according to the evidence. Nothing herein shall be construed to disallow the usual challenges in law to the whole jury so sworn or to any juror; and if by reason of such challenge any juror is withdrawn from a jury being selected to try a case, his place on that jury shall be taken by another qualified juror. The presiding judge shall decide all questions as to the competency of jurors. (1790, c. 321, P.R.; 1822, c. 1133, s. 1, P.R.; R.C., c. 31, s. 34; Code, s. 405; Rev., s. 1966; C.S., s. 2324; 1967, c. 218, s. 1; 2013-164, s. 1.)

§ 9-15. Questioning jurors without challenge; challenges for cause.

(a) The court, and any party to an action, or his counsel of record shall be allowed, in selecting the jury, to make direct oral inquiry of any prospective juror as to the fitness and competency of any person to serve as a juror, without having such inquiry treated as a challenge of such person, and it shall not be considered by the court that any person is challenged as a juror until the party shall formally state that such person is so challenged.

(b) It shall not be a valid cause for challenge that any juror, regular or supplemental, is not a freeholder or has not paid the taxes assessed against him.

(c) In civil cases if any juror has a suit pending and at issue in the court in which he is serving, he may be challenged for cause, and he shall be withdrawn from the trial panel, and may be withdrawn from the venire in the discretion of the presiding judge. In criminal cases challenges are governed by Article 72,

Selecting and Impaneling the Jury, of Chapter 15A of the General Statutes. (1806, c. 694, P.R.; 1868-9, c. 9, s. 7; Code, s. 1728; Rev., s. 1960; 1913, c. 31, ss. 5, 6, 7; C.S., ss. 2316, 2325, 2326; 1933, c. 130; 1967, c. 218, s. 1; 1973, c. 95; 1977, c. 711, s. 11.)

§ 9-16. Exemption from civil arrest.

No sheriff or other officer shall arrest under civil process any juror during his attendance at or going to and returning from any session of the superior or district court. Any such arrest shall be invalid, and the defendant on motion shall be discharged. (1779, c. 157, s. 10, P.R.; R.C., c. 31, s. 31; Code, s. 1735; Rev., s. 1979, C.S., s. 2328; 1967, c. 218, s. 1.)

§ 9-17. Jurors impaneled to try case furnished with accommodations; separation of jurors.

A jury, impaneled to try any cause, shall be put in charge of an officer of the court and shall be furnished with such accommodations as the court may order, and the accommodations shall be paid for by the parties or by the State, as ordered by the presiding judge. When sequestration of the jury is ordered in a criminal case, however, the State shall pay for all accommodations of jurors.

The presiding judge, in his discretion, may direct any jury to be sequestered while it has a case or issue under consideration. (1876-7, c. 173; Code, s. 1736; 1889, c. 44; Rev., s. 1978, C.S., s. 2327; 1947, c. 1007, s. 2; 1967, c. 218, s. 1; 1977, c. 711, s. 12.)

§ 9-18. Alternate jurors.

(a)   Civil Cases. Whenever the presiding judge deems it appropriate, one or more alternate jurors may be selected in the same manner as the regular trial panel of jurors in the case. Each party shall be entitled to two peremptory challenges as to each such alternate juror, in addition to any unexpended challenges the party may have after the selection of the regular trial panel. Alternate jurors shall be sworn and seated near the jury with equal opportunity to see and hear the proceedings and shall attend the trial at all times with the jury and shall obey all orders and admonitions of the court to the jury. When the jurors are ordered kept together in any case, the alternate jurors shall be kept with them. An alternate juror shall receive the same compensation as other jurors and, except as hereinafter provided, shall be discharged upon the final submission of the case to the jury. If before that time any juror dies, becomes incapacitated or disqualified, or is discharged for any reason, an alternate juror shall become a part of the jury and serve in all respects as those selected on the regular trial panel. If more than one alternate juror has been selected, they shall be available to become a part of the jury in the order in which they were selected.

(b) Criminal Cases. Procedures relating to alternate jurors in criminal cases are governed by Article 72, Selecting and Impaneling the Jury, of Chapter 15A of the General Statutes. (1931, c. 103; 1939, c. 35; 1951, cc. 82, 1043; 1967, c. 218, s. 1; 1977, c. 406, ss. 3-5; c. 711, s. 13; 1979, c. 711, s. 2.)

Article 3.

Peremptory Challenges.

§ 9-19. Peremptory challenges in civil cases.

The clerk, before a jury is impaneled to try the issues in any civil suit, shall read over the names of the prospective jurors in the presence and hearing of the parties or their counsel; and the parties, or their counsel for them, may challenge peremptorily eight jurors without showing any cause therefor, and the challenges shall be allowed by the court. (1796, c. 452, s. 2, P.R.; 1812, c. 833, P.R.; R.C., c. 31, s. 35; Code, s. 406; Rev., s. 1964; C.S., s. 2331; 1935, c. 475, s. 1; 1965, c. 1182; 1967, c. 218, s. 1.)

§ 9-20. Civil cases having several plaintiffs or several defendants; challenges apportioned; discretion of judge.

(a) When there are two or more defendants in a civil action, the presiding judge, if it appears that there are antagonistic interests between the defendants, may in the judge's discretion apportion among the defendants the challenges now allowed by law, or the judge may increase the number of challenges to not exceeding six for each defendant or class of defendants representing the same interest.

(b) When there are two or more plaintiffs in a civil action, the presiding judge, if it appears that there are antagonistic interests between the plaintiffs, may, in the judge's discretion, apportion among the plaintiffs the challenges now allowed by law, or the judge may increase the number of challenges to not exceeding six for each plaintiff or class of plaintiffs representing the same interest.

(c) Whenever a judge exercises the discretion authorized by subsection (a) or (b) of this section to increase the number of challenges for either the plaintiffs or the defendants, the judge may, in the judge's discretion, increase the number of challenges for the opposing side, not to exceed the total number given to the other side. (1905, c. 357; Rev., s. 1965; C.S., s. 2332; 1967, c. 218, s. 1; 2007-210, s. 1.)

§ 9-21. Peremptory challenges in criminal cases governed by Chapter 15A.

Peremptory challenges in criminal cases are governed by Article 72, Selecting and Impaneling the Jury, of Chapter 15A of the General Statutes. (22 Hen. VIII, c. 14, s. 6; 33 Edw. I, c. 4; 1777, c. 115, s. 85, P.R.; 1801, c. 592, s. 1, P.R.; 1812, c. 833, P.R.; 1826, c. 9; 1827, c. 10; R.S., c. 35, ss. 19, 21; R.C., c. 35, ss. 32, 33; 1871-2, c. 39; Code, ss. 1199, 1200; 1887, c. 53; Rev., ss. 3263, 3264; 1907, c. 415; 1913, c. 31, ss. 3, 4; C.S., ss. 4633, 4634; 1935, c. 475, ss. 2, 3; 1967, c. 218, s. 1; 1969, c. 205, s. 7; 1971, c. 75; 1977, c. 711, s. 14.)

Article 4.

Grand Jurors.

§§ 9-22 through 9-26. Repealed by Session Laws 1973, c. 1286, s. 26.

§§ 9-27 through 9-31. Repealed by Session Laws 1967, c. 218, s. 1.

Article 5.

Discharge of Jurors Prohibited.

§ 9-32. Discharge of juror unlawful.

(a) No employer may discharge or demote any employee because the employee has been called for jury duty, or is serving as a grand juror or petit juror.

(b) Any employer who violates any provision of this section shall be liable in a civil action for reasonable damages suffered by an employee as a result of the violation, and an employee discharged or demoted in violation of this section shall be entitled to be reinstated to his former position. The burden of proof shall be upon the employee.

(c) The statute of limitations for actions under this section shall be one year pursuant to G.S. 1-54. (1987, c. 702, s. 1.)

Chapter 10.

Notaries.

§§ 10-1 through 10-18: Repealed by Session Laws 1991, c. 683, s. 1.

Chapter 10A.

Notaries.

§§ 10A-1 through 10A-17: Repealed by Session Laws 2005-391, s. 3, effective December 1, 2005, and applicable to notarial acts and applications for notary commissions and recommissions made on or after that date.

Chapter 10B.

Notaries.

Article 1.

Notary Public Act.

Part 1. General Provisions.

§ 10B-1. Short title.

This Article is the "Notary Public Act" and may be cited by that name. (1991, c. 683, s. 2; 2005-391, s. 4.)

§ 10B-2. Purposes.

This Chapter shall be construed and applied to advance its underlying purposes, which are the following:

(1)   To promote, serve, and protect the public interests.

(2)   To simplify, clarify, and modernize the law governing notaries.

(3)   To prevent fraud and forgery.

(4)   To foster ethical conduct among notaries.

(5)   To enhance interstate recognition of notarial acts.

(6)   To integrate procedures for traditional paper and electronic notarial acts. (1991, c. 683, s. 2; 1998-228, s. 1; 2005-391, s. 4.)

§ 10B-3. Definitions.

The following definitions apply in this Chapter:

(1)   Acknowledgment. - A notarial act in which a notary certifies that at a single time and place all of the following occurred:

a.   An individual appeared in person before the notary and presented a record.

b.   The individual was personally known to the notary or identified by the notary through satisfactory evidence.

c.   The individual did either of the following:

i.   Indicated to the notary that the signature on the record was the individual's signature.

ii. Signed the record while in the physical presence of the notary and while being personally observed signing the record by the notary.

(2) Affirmation. - A notarial act which is legally equivalent to an oath and in which a notary certifies that at a single time and place all of the following occurred:

a. An individual appeared in person before the notary.

b. The individual was personally known to the notary or identified by the notary through satisfactory evidence.

c. The individual made a vow of truthfulness on penalty of perjury, based on personal honor and without invoking a deity or using any form of the word "swear".

(3) Attest or attestation. - The completion of a certificate by a notary who has performed a notarial act.

(4) Commission. - The empowerment to perform notarial acts and the written evidence of authority to perform those acts.

(5) Credible witness. - An individual who is personally known to the notary and to whom all of the following also apply:

a. The notary believes the individual to be honest and reliable for the purpose of confirming to the notary the identity of another individual.

b. The notary believes the individual is not a party to or beneficiary of the transaction.

(6) Department. - The North Carolina Department of the Secretary of State.

(7) Director. - The Division Director for the North Carolina Department of the Secretary of State Notary Public Section.

(8) Jurat. - A notary's certificate evidencing the administration of an oath or affirmation.

(9) Moral turpitude. - Conduct contrary to expected standards of honesty, morality, or integrity.

(10) Nickname. - A descriptive, familiar, or shortened form of a proper name.

(11) Notarial act, notary act, and notarization. - The act of taking an acknowledgment, taking a verification or proof or administering an oath or affirmation that a notary is empowered to perform under G.S. 10B-20(a).

(12) Notarial certificate and certificate. - The portion of a notarized record that is completed by the notary, bears the notary's signature and seal, and states the facts attested by the notary in a particular notarization.

(13) Notary public and notary. - A person commissioned to perform notarial acts under this Chapter. A notary is a public officer of the State of North Carolina and shall act in full and strict compliance with this act.

(14) Oath. - A notarial act which is legally equivalent to an affirmation and in which a notary certifies that at a single time and place all of the following occurred:

a. An individual appeared in person before the notary.

b. The individual was personally known to the notary or identified by the notary through satisfactory evidence.

c. The individual made a vow of truthfulness on penalty of perjury while invoking a deity or using any form of the word "swear".

(15) Official misconduct. - Either of the following:

a. A notary's performance of a prohibited act or failure to perform a mandated act set forth in this Chapter or any other law in connection with notarization.

b. A notary's performance of a notarial act in a manner found by the Secretary to be negligent or against the public interest.

(16) Personal appearance and appear in person before a notary. - An individual and a notary are in close physical proximity to one another so that they may freely see and communicate with one another and exchange records back and forth during the notarization process.

(17) Personal knowledge or personally know. - Familiarity with an individual resulting from interactions with that individual over a period of time sufficient to eliminate every reasonable doubt that the individual has the identity claimed.

(18) Principal. - One of the following:

a. In the case of an acknowledgment, the individual whose identity and due execution of a record is being certified by the notary.

b. In the case of a verification or proof, the individual other than a subscribing witness, whose:

i. Identity and due execution of the record is being proven; or

ii. Signature is being identified as genuine.

c. In the case of an oath or affirmation, the individual who makes a vow of truthfulness on penalty of perjury.

(19) Record. - Information that is inscribed on a tangible medium and called a traditional or paper record.

(20) Regular place of work or business. - A location, office or other workspace, where an individual regularly spends all or part of the individual's work time.

(21) Revocation. - The cancellation of the notary's commission stated in the order of revocation.

(22) Satisfactory evidence. - Identification of an individual based on either of the following:

a. At least one current document issued by a federal, state, or federal or state-recognized tribal government agency bearing the photographic image of the individual's face and either the signature or a physical description of the individual.

b. The oath or affirmation of one credible witness who personally knows the individual seeking to be identified.

(23) Seal or stamp. - A device for affixing on a paper record an image containing a notary's name, the words "notary public," and other information as required in G.S. 10B-37.

(24) Secretary. - The North Carolina Secretary of State or the Secretary's designee.

(25) Repealed by Session Laws 2006-59, s. 1, effective October 1, 2006, except as otherwise set forth in the act, and applicable to notarial acts performed on or after October 1, 2006.

(26) Subscribing witness. - A person who signs a record for the purpose of being a witness to the principal's execution of the record or to the principal's acknowledgment of his or her execution of the record. A subscribing witness may give proof of the execution of the record as provided in subdivision (28) of this section.

(27) Suspension and restriction. - The termination of a notary's commission for a period of time stated in an order of restriction or suspension. The terms "restriction" or "suspension" or a combination of both terms shall be used synonymously.

(28) Verification or proof. - A notarial act in which a notary certifies that all of the following occurred:

a. An individual appeared in person before the notary.

b. The individual was personally known to the notary or identified by the notary through satisfactory evidence.

c. The individual was not a party to or beneficiary of the transaction.

d. The individual took an oath or gave an affirmation and testified to one of the following:

i. The individual is a subscribing witness and the principal who signed the record did so while being personally observed by the subscribing witness.

ii. The individual is a subscribing witness and the principal who signed the record acknowledged his or her signature to the subscribing witness.

iii. The individual recognized either the signature on the record of the principal or the signature on the record of the subscribing witness and the signature was genuine. (1991, c. 683, s. 2; 1998-228, s. 2; 2005-391, s. 4; 2006-59, s. 1.)

§ 10B-4: Reserved for future codification purposes.

Part 2. Commissioning.

§ 10B-5. Qualifications.

(a) Except as provided in subsection (d) of this section, the Secretary shall commission as a notary any qualified person who submits an application in accordance with this Chapter.

(b) A person qualified for a notarial commission shall meet all of the following requirements:

(1) Be at least 18 years of age or legally emancipated as defined in Article 35 of Chapter 7B of the General Statutes.

(2) Reside or have a regular place of work or business in this State.

(3) Reside legally in the United States.

(4) Speak, read, and write the English language.

(5) Possess a high school diploma or equivalent.

(6) Pass the course of instruction described in this Article, unless the person is a licensed member of the North Carolina State Bar.

(7) Purchase and keep as a reference the most recent manual approved by the Secretary that describes the duties and authority of notaries public.

(8) Submit an application containing no significant misstatement or omission of fact. The application form shall be provided by the Secretary and be available at the register of deeds office in each county. Every application shall include the signature of the applicant written with pen and ink, and the signature

shall be acknowledged by the applicant before a person authorized to administer oaths.

(9) Repealed by Session Laws 2013-204, s. 1, effective July 1, 2013.

(c) The notary shall be commissioned in his or her county of residence, unless the notary is not a North Carolina resident, in which case he or she shall be commissioned in the county of his or her employment or business.

(d) The Secretary may deny an application for commission or recommission if any of the following apply to an applicant:

(1) Submission of an incomplete application or an application containing material misstatement or omission of fact.

(2) The applicant's conviction or plea of admission or nolo contendere to a felony or any crime involving dishonesty or moral turpitude. In no case may a commission be issued to an applicant within 10 years after release from prison, probation, or parole, whichever is later.

(3) A finding or admission of liability against the applicant in a civil lawsuit based on the applicant's deceit.

(4) The revocation, suspension, restriction, or denial of a notarial commission or professional license by this or any other state or nation. In no case may a commission be issued to an applicant within five years after the completion of all conditions of any disciplinary order.

(5) A finding that the applicant has engaged in official misconduct, whether or not disciplinary action resulted.

(6) An applicant knowingly using false or misleading advertising in which the applicant as a notary represents that the applicant has powers, duties, rights, or privileges that the applicant does not possess by law.

(7) A finding by a state bar or court that the applicant has engaged in the unauthorized practice of law. (Code, ss. 3304, 3305; Rev., ss. 2347, 2348; C.S., s. 3172; 1927, c. 117; 1959, c. 1161, s. 2; 1969, c. 563, s. 1; c. 912, s. 1; 1973, c. 680, s. 1; 1983, c. 427, ss. 1, 2; c. 713, s. 22; 1991, c. 683, s. 2; 1995, c. 226, s. 1; 1998-228, s. 3; 1999-337, s.3(a); 2001-450, s. 1; 2002-126, s.

29A.21; 2005-75, s. 1. ; 2005-391, s. 4; 2006-59, s. 2; 2009-227, s. 1; 2013-204, s. 1.)

§ 10B-6. Application for commission.

Every application for a notary commission shall be made on paper with original signatures, or in another form determined by the Secretary, and shall include all of the following:

(1) A statement of the applicant's personal qualifications as required by this Chapter.

(2) A certificate or signed statement by the instructor evidencing successful completion of the course of instruction as required by this Chapter.

(3) A notarized declaration of the applicant, as required by this Chapter.

(4) Any other information that the Secretary deems appropriate.

(5) The application fee required by this Chapter. (2005-391, s. 4.)

§ 10B-7. Statement of personal qualification.

(a) The application for a notary commission shall include at least all of the following:

(1) The applicant's full legal name and the name to be used for commissioning, excluding nicknames.

(2) The applicant's date of birth.

(3) The mailing address for the applicant's residence, the street address for the applicant's residence, and the telephone number for the applicant's residence.

(4) The applicant's county of residence.

(5) The name of the applicant's employer, the street and mailing address for the applicant's employer, and telephone number for the applicant's employer.

(6)   The applicant's last four digits of the applicant's social security number.

(7)   The applicant's personal and business e-mail addresses.

(8)   A declaration that the applicant is a citizen of the United States or proof of the applicant's legal residency in this country.

(9)   A declaration that the applicant can speak, read, and writes in the English language.

(10)   A complete listing of any issuances, denials, revocations, suspensions, restrictions, and resignations of a notarial commission, professional license, or public office involving the applicant in this or any other state or nation.

(11)   A complete listing of any criminal convictions of the applicant, including any pleas of admission or nolo contendere, in this or any other state or nation.

(12)   A complete listing of any civil findings or admissions of fault or liability regarding the applicant's activities as a notary, in this or any other state or nation.

(b)   The information provided in an application that relates to subdivisions (2), (3), (6), and (7) of subsection (a) of this section shall be considered confidential information and shall not be subject to disclosure under Chapter 132 of the General Statutes. (2005-391, s. 4; 2006-59, s. 3.)

§ 10B-8. Course of study and examination.

(a)   Every applicant for an initial notary commission shall, within the three months preceding application, take a course of classroom instruction of not less than six hours approved by the Secretary and take a written examination approved by the Secretary. An applicant must answer at least eighty percent (80%) of the questions correctly in order to pass the exam. This subsection shall not apply to a licensed member of the North Carolina State Bar.

(b)   Every applicant for recommissioning shall pass a written examination approved by and administered by or under the direction of the Secretary, unless the person is a licensed member of the North Carolina State Bar.

(c) The content of the course of instruction and the written examinations shall be notarial laws, procedures, and ethics.

(d) The Secretary may charge such fees as are reasonably necessary to pay the cost associated with developing and administering examinations permitted by this Chapter and for conducting the training of notaries and notary instructors. (2005-391, s. 4.)

§ 10B-9. Length of term and jurisdiction.

A person commissioned under this Chapter may perform notarial acts in any part of this State for a term of five years, unless the commission is earlier revoked or resigned. No commissions shall be effective prior to the administration of the oath of office. Any notarial acts performed before the administration of the oath of office, either the original commissioning or recommissioning, are invalid. (1891, c. 248; Rev., s. 2351; c.s., s. 3176; 1973, c. 680, s. 1; 1991, c. 683, s. 2; 2005-391, s. 4.)

§ 10B-10. Commission; oath of office.

(a) If the Secretary grants a commission to an applicant, the Secretary shall notify the appointee and shall instruct the appointee regarding the proper procedure for taking the oath at the register of deeds office in the county of the appointee's commissioning.

(b) The appointee shall appear before the register of deeds no later than 45 days after commissioning and shall be duly qualified by taking the general oath of office prescribed in G.S. 11-11 and the oath prescribed for officers in G.S. 11-7.

(c) After the appointee qualifies by taking the oath of office required under subsection (b) of this section, the register of deeds shall place the notary record in a book designated for that purpose, or the notary record may be recorded in the Consolidated Document Book and indexed in the Consolidated Real Property Index under the notary's name in the grantor index. The notary record may be kept in electronic format so long as the signature of the notary public may be viewed and printed. The notary record shall contain the name and the signature of the notary as commissioned, the effective date and expiration date of the commission, the date the oath was administered, and the date of any restriction, suspension, revocation, or resignation. The record shall constitute the official record of the qualification of notaries public.

(d) The register of deeds shall deliver the commission to the notary following completion of the requirements of this section and shall notify the Secretary of the delivery.

(e) If the appointee does not appear before the register of deeds within 45 days of commissioning, the register of deeds must return the commission to the Secretary, and the appointee must reapply for commissioning. If the appointee reapplies within one year of the granting of the commission, the Secretary may waive the educational requirements of this Chapter. (Code, ss. 3304, 3305; Rev., ss. 2347, 2348; C.S., s. 3173; 1969,c. 912, s. 2; 1973, c. 680, s. 1; 1991, c. 683, s. 2; 2005-391, s. 4; 2006-59, s. 4.)

§ 10B-11. Recommissioning.

(a) A commissioned notary may apply for recommissioning no earlier than 10 weeks prior to the expiration date of the notary's commission.

(b) A notary whose commission has not expired must comply with the following requirements to be recommissioned:

(1) Submit a new application meeting the requirements of G.S. 10B-6, except for G.S. 10B-6(2).

(2) Meet all the requirements of G.S. 10B-5(b), except for G.S. 10B-5(b)(5), (6), and (9).

(3) Achieve a passing score on the written examination required under G.S. 10B-8(b). This requirement does not apply if the notary is a licensed member of the North Carolina State Bar, or if the notary has been continuously commissioned in North Carolina since July 10, 1991, and has never been disciplined by the Secretary.

(c) An individual may apply for recommissioning within one year after the expiration of the individual's commission. The individual must comply with the requirement of subsection (b) of this section. The individual must also fulfill the educational requirement under G.S. 10B-8(a), unless the Secretary waives that requirement. (1991, c. 683, s. 2; 1995, c. 226, s. 2; 2005-391, s. 4; 2006-59, s. 5.)

§ 10B-12. Notarized declaration.

The application for a notary public commission shall contain the following declaration to be executed by each applicant under oath:

Declaration of Applicant

I, _____ (name of applicant), solemnly swear or affirm under penalty of perjury that the information in this application is true, complete, and correct; that I understand the official duties and responsibilities of a notary public in this State, as described in the statutes; and that I will perform to the best of my ability all notarial acts in accordance with the law.

_____

(signature of applicant)

(2005-391, s. 4.)

§ 10B-13. Application fee.

Every applicant for a notary commission shall pay to the Secretary a nonrefundable application fee of fifty dollars ($50.00). (2005-391, s. 4.)

§ 10B-14. Instructor's certification.

(a) The course of study required by G.S. 10B-5(b) shall be taught by an instructor certified under rules adopted by the Secretary. An instructor must meet the following requirements to be certified to teach a course of study for notaries public:

(1) Complete and pass an instructor certification course of not less than six hours taught by the Director or other person approved by the Secretary.

(2) Have at least one year of active experience as a notary public.

(3) Maintain a current commission as a notary public.

(4) Possess the current notary public guidebook.

(5) Pay a nonrefundable fee of fifty dollars ($50.00).

(b) Certification to teach a course of study for notaries shall be effective for two years. A certification may be renewed by passing a recertification course taught by the Director or other person approved by the Secretary and by paying a nonrefundable fee of fifty dollars ($50.00).

(c) The following individuals may be certified to teach a course of study for notaries public without paying the fee required by this section, and they may renew their certification without paying the renewal fee, so long as they remain actively employed in the capacities named:

(1) Registers of deeds.

(2) Clerks of court.

(3) The Director and other duly authorized employees of the Secretary.

(d) Former registers of deeds and clerks of court who have been certified as notary public instructors must apply for commissioning as a notary public but are exempt from the education requirements of G.S. 10B-8 after successful completion of an examination administered by the Secretary.

(e) Assistant and deputy registers of deeds and assistant and deputy clerks of court must have a regular notary commission prior to receiving a certification or recertification as a notary public instructor.

(f) The Secretary may suspend or revoke the certification of a notary instructor for violating the provisions of this Chapter or any of the administrative rules implementing it. (1991, c. 683, s. 2; 1998-212, s. 29A.9(a); 1998-228, s. 4; 1999-337, s. 3(b); 2005-391, s. 4.)

§ 10B-15: Reserved for future codification purposes.

§ 10B-16: Reserved for future codification purposes.

§ 10B-17: Reserved for future codification purposes.

§ 10B-18: Reserved for future codification purposes.

§ 10B-19: Reserved for future codification purposes.

Part 3. Notarial Acts, Powers, and Limitations.

§ 10B-20. Powers and limitations.

(a)   A notary may perform any of the following notarial acts:

(1)   Acknowledgments.

(2)   Oaths and affirmations.

(3)   Repealed by Session Laws 2006-59, s. 6, effective October 1, 2006, and except as otherwise set forth in the act, applicable to notarial acts performed on or after October 1, 2006.

(4)   Verifications or proofs.

(b)   A notarial act shall be attested by all of the following:

(1)   The signature of the notary, exactly as shown on the notary's commission.

(2)   The legible appearance of the notary's name exactly as shown on the notary's commission. The legible appearance of the name may be ascertained from the notary's typed or printed name near the notary's signature or from elsewhere in the notarial certificate or from the notary's seal if the name is legible.

(3)   The clear and legible appearance of the notary's stamp or seal.

(4) A statement of the date the notary's commission expires. The statement of the date that the notary's commission expires may appear in the notary's stamp or seal or elsewhere in the notarial certificate.

(c) A notary shall not perform a notarial act if any of the following apply:

(1) The principal or subscribing witness is not in the notary's presence at the time the notarial act is performed. However, nothing in this Chapter shall require a notary to complete the notarial certificate attesting to the notarial act in the presence of the principal or subscribing witness.

(2) The principal or subscribing witness is not personally known to the notary or identified by the notary through satisfactory evidence.

(2a) The credible witness is not personally known to the notary.

(3), (4) Repealed by Session Laws 2006-59, s. 8, effective October 1, 2006, and except as otherwise set forth in the act, applicable to notarial acts performed on or after October 1, 2006.

(5) The notary is a signer of, party to, or beneficiary of the record, that is to be notarized. However, a disqualification under this subdivision shall not apply to a notary who is named in a record solely as (i) the trustee in a deed of trust, (ii) the drafter of the record, (iii) the person to whom a registered document should be mailed or sent after recording, or (iv) the attorney for a party to the record, so long as the notary is not also a party to the record individually or in some other representative or fiduciary capacity. A notary who is an employee of a party shall not be disqualified under this subdivision solely because of the notary's employment by a party to the record or solely because the notary owns stock in a party to the record.

(6) The notary will receive directly from a transaction connected with the notarial act any commission, fee, advantage, right, title, interest, cash, property, or other consideration exceeding in value the fees specified in G.S. 10B-31, other than fees or other consideration paid for services rendered by a licensed attorney, a licensed real estate broker or salesperson, a motor vehicle dealer, or a banker.

(d) A notary may certify the affixation of a signature by mark on a record presented for notarization if:

(1) The mark is affixed in the presence of the notary;

(2) The notary writes below the mark: "Mark affixed by (name of signer by mark) in presence of undersigned notary"; and

(3) The notary notarizes the signature by performing an acknowledgment, oath or affirmation, jurat, or verification or proof.

(e) If a principal is physically unable to sign or make a mark on a record presented for notarization, that principal may designate another person as his or her designee, who shall be a disinterested party, to sign on the principal's behalf pursuant to the following procedure:

(1) The principal directs the designee to sign the record in the presence of the notary and two witnesses unaffected by the record;

(2) The designee signs the principal's name in the presence of the principal, the notary, and the two witnesses;

(3) Both witnesses sign their own names to the record near the principal's signature;

(4) The notary writes below the principal's signature: "Signature affixed by designee in the presence of (names and addresses of principal and witnesses)"; and

(5) The notary notarizes the signature through an acknowledgment, oath or affirmation, jurat, or verification or proof.

(f) A notarial act performed in another jurisdiction in compliance with the laws of that jurisdiction is valid to the same extent as if it had been performed by a notary commissioned under this Chapter if the notarial act is performed by a notary public of that jurisdiction or by any person authorized to perform notarial acts in that jurisdiction under the laws of that jurisdiction, the laws of this State, or federal law.

(g) Persons authorized by federal law or regulation to perform notarial acts may perform the acts for persons serving in or with the Armed Forces of the United States, their spouses, and their dependents.

(h) The Secretary and register of deeds in the county in which a notary qualified may certify to the commission of the notary.

(i) A notary public who is not an attorney licensed to practice law in this State who advertises the person's services as a notary public in a language other than English, by radio, television, signs, pamphlets, newspapers, other written communication, or in any other manner, shall post or otherwise include with the advertisement the notice set forth in this subsection in English and in the language used for the advertisement. The notice shall be of conspicuous size, if in writing, and shall state: "I AM NOT AN ATTORNEY LICENSED TO PRACTICE LAW IN THE STATE OF NORTH CAROLINA, AND I MAY NOT GIVE LEGAL ADVICE OR ACCEPT FEES FOR LEGAL ADVICE." If the advertisement is by radio or television, the statement may be modified but must include substantially the same message.

(j) A notary public who is not an attorney licensed to practice law in this State is prohibited from representing or advertising that the notary public is an "immigration consultant" or expert on immigration matters unless the notary public is an accredited representative of an organization recognized by the Board of Immigration Appeals pursuant to Title 8, Part 292, section 2(a-e) of the Code of Federal Regulations (8 C.F.R. § 292.2(a-e)).

(k) A notary public who is not an attorney licensed to practice law in this State is prohibited from rendering any service that constitutes the unauthorized practice of law. A nonattorney notary shall not assist another person in drafting, completing, selecting, or understanding a record or transaction requiring a notarial act.

(l) A notary public required to comply with the provisions of subsection (i) of this section shall prominently post at the notary public's place of business a schedule of fees established by law, which a notary public may charge. The fee schedule shall be written in English and in the non-English language in which the notary services were solicited and shall contain the notice required in subsection (i) of this section, unless the notice is otherwise prominently posted at the notary public's place of business.

(m) If notarial certificate wording is not provided or indicated for a record, a notary who is not also a licensed attorney shall not determine the type of notarial act or certificate to be used. This does not prohibit a notary from offering the selection of certificate forms recognized in this Chapter or as otherwise authorized by law.

(n) A notary shall not claim to have powers, qualifications, rights, or privileges that the office of notary does not provide, including the power to counsel on immigration matters.

(o) Before signing a notarial certificate and except as provided in this subsection, a notary shall cross out or mark through all blank lines or spaces in the certificate. However:

(1) Notwithstanding the provisions of this section, a notary shall not be required to complete, cross out, or mark through blank lines or spaces in the notary certificate form provided for in G.S. 47-43 indicating when and where a power of attorney is recorded if that recording information is not known to the notary at the time the notary completes and signs the certificate;

(2) A notary's failure to cross out or mark through blank lines or spaces in a notarial certificate shall not affect the sufficiency, validity, or enforceability of the certificate or the related record; and

(3) A notary's failure to cross out or mark through blank lines or spaces in a notarial certificate shall not be grounds for a register of deeds to refuse to accept a record for registration. (1866, c. 30; 1879, c. 128; Code, s. 3307; Rev., ss. 2350, 2351a, 2352; C.S., ss. 3175, 3177, 3179; 1951, c. 1006, s. 1; 1953, c. 836; 1961, c. 733; 1967, c. 24, s. 22; c. 984; 1973, c. 680, s. 1; 1977, c. 375, s. 5; 1991, c. 683, s. 2; 1998-228, s. 5; 2001-450, s. 2; 2001-487, s. 121; 2005-391, s. 4; 2006-59, ss. 6-12; 2006-199, s. 1; 2011-183, s. 7; 2013-204, s. 1.1.)

§ 10B-21. Notaries ex officio.

(a) The clerks of the superior court may act as notaries public in their several counties by virtue of their offices as clerks and may certify their notarial acts only under the seals of their respective courts. Assistant and deputy clerks of superior court, by virtue of their offices, may perform the following notarial acts and may certify these notarial acts only under the seals of their respective courts:

(1) Oaths and affirmations.

(2) Verifications or proofs.

Upon completion of the course of study provided for in G.S. 10B-5(b), assistant and deputy clerks of superior court may, by virtue of their offices, perform all other notarial acts and may certify these notarial acts only under the seals of their respective courts. A course of study attended only by assistant and deputy clerks of superior court may be taught at any mutually convenient location agreed to by the Secretary and the Administrative Office of the Courts.

(b) Registers of deeds may act as notaries public in their several counties by virtue of their offices as registers of deeds and may certify their notarial acts only under the seals of their respective offices. Assistant and deputy registers of deeds, by virtue of their offices, may perform the following notarial acts and may certify these notarial acts only under the seals of their respective offices:

(1) Oaths and affirmations.

(2) Verifications or proofs.

Upon completion of the course of study provided for in G.S. 10B-5(b), assistant and deputy registers of deeds may, by virtue of their offices, perform all other notarial acts and may certify these notarial acts only under the seals of their respective offices. A course of study attended only by assistant and deputy registers of deeds may be taught at any mutually convenient location agreed to by the Secretary and the North Carolina Association of Registers of Deeds.

(c) The Director may act as a notary public by virtue of the Director's employment in the Department of the Secretary and may certify a notarial act performed in that capacity under the seal of the Secretary.

(d) Unless otherwise provided by law, a person designated a notary public by this section may charge a fee for a notarial act performed in accordance with G.S. 10B-31. The fee authorized by this section is payable to the governmental unit or agency by whom the person is employed.

(e) Nothing in this section shall authorize a person to act as a notary public other than in the performance of the official duties of the person's office unless the person complies fully with the requirements of G.S. 10B-5. (1833, c. 7, ss. 1, 2; R.C., c. 75, s. 3; Code, s. 3306; Rev., s. 2349; C.S., s. 3174; 1973, c. 680, s. 1; 1991, c. 683, s. 2; 1998-228, s. 8.; 2005-391, s. 4.)

§ 10B-22. False certificate; foreign language certificates.

(a) A notary shall not execute a notarial certificate containing information known or believed by the notary to be false.

(b) A notary shall not execute a certificate that is not written in the English language. A notary may execute a certificate written in the English language that accompanies a record written in another language, which record may include a translation of the notarial certificate into the other language. In those instances, the notary shall execute only the English language certificate. (2005-391, s. 4.)

§ 10B-23. Improper records.

(a) A notary shall not notarize a signature on a record without a notarial certificate indicating what type of notarial act was performed. However, a notary may administer an oath or affirmation without completing a jurat.

(b) A notary shall neither certify, notarize, nor authenticate a photograph. A notary may notarize an affidavit regarding and attached to a photograph. (2005-391, s. 4; 2006-59, s. 13.)

§ 10B-24. Testimonials.

A notary shall not use the official notary title or seal in a manner intended to endorse, promote, denounce, or oppose any product, service, contest, candidate, or other offering. This section does not prohibit a notary public from performing a notarial act upon a record executed by another individual. (2005-391, s. 4.)

§ 10B-25: Reserved for future codification purposes.

§ 10B-26: Reserved for future codification purposes.

§ 10B-27: Reserved for future codification purposes.

§ 10B-28: Reserved for future codification purposes.

§ 10B-29: Reserved for future codification purposes.

Part 4. Fees.

§ 10B-30. Imposition and waiver of fees.

(a)   For performing a notarial act, a notary may charge up to the maximum fee specified in this Chapter.

(b)   A notary shall not discriminatorily condition the fee for a notarial act on any attribute of the principal that would constitute unlawful discrimination.

(c)   Nothing in this Chapter shall compel a notary to charge a fee.

(d)   A notary may not charge any fee for witnessing and affixing a notarial seal to an absentee ballot application or certificate under G.S. 163-231. (2005-391, s. 4; 2013-381, s. 4.7.)

§ 10B-31. Fees for notarial acts.

The maximum fees that may be charged by a notary for notarial acts are as follows:

(1)   For acknowledgments, jurats, verifications or proofs, five dollars ($5.00) per principal signature.

(2)   For oaths or affirmations without a signature, five dollars ($5.00) per person, except for an oath or affirmation administered to a credible witness to vouch for the identity of a principal or subscribing witness. (Code, s. 3749; 1889, c. 446; 1895, c. 296; 1903, c. 734; Rev., s. 2800; C.S., s. 3178; 1973, c. 680, s. 1; 1977, c. 429, ss. 1, 2; 1981, c. 872; 1991, c. 683, s. 2; 1998-228, s. 6; 2005-328, s. 1; 2005-391, s. 4; 2006-59, s. 14.)

§ 10B-32. Notice of fees.

Notaries who charge for their notarial services shall conspicuously display in their places of business, or present to each principal outside their places of business, an English-language schedule of fees for notarial acts. No part of any notarial fee schedule shall be printed in smaller than 10-point type. (2005-391, s. 4.)

§ 10B-33: Reserved for future codification purposes.

§ 10B-34: Reserved for future codification purposes.

Part 5. Signature and Seal.

§ 10B-35. Official signature.

When notarizing a paper record, a notary shall sign by hand in ink on the notarial certificate. The notary shall comply with the requirements of G.S. 10B-20(b)(1) and (b)(2). The notary shall affix the official signature only after the notarial act is performed. The notary shall not sign a paper record using the facsimile stamp or an electronic or other printing method. (2005-391, s. 4; 2006-59, s. 15.)

§ 10B-36. Official seal.

(a) A notary shall keep an official seal or stamp that is the exclusive property of the notary. The notary shall keep the seal in a secure location. A notary shall not allow another person to use or possess the seal, and shall not surrender the seal to the notary's employer upon termination of employment.

(b) The seal shall be affixed only after the notarial act is performed. The notary shall place the image or impression of the seal near the notary's signature on every paper record notarized. The seal and the notary's signature shall appear on the same page of a record as the text of the notarial certificate.

(c) A notary shall do the following within 10 days of discovering that the notary's seal has been lost or stolen:

(1) Inform the appropriate law enforcement agency in the case of theft or vandalism.

(2) Notify the appropriate register of deeds and the Secretary in writing and signed in the official name in which he or she was commissioned.

(d) As soon as is reasonably practicable after resignation, revocation, or expiration of a notary commission, or death of the notary, the seal shall be delivered to the Secretary for disposal. (1973, c. 680, s. 1; 1991, c. 683, s. 2; 1998-228, s. 7; 2005-391, s. 4; 2006-59, s. 16.)

§ 10B-37. Seal image.

(a) A notary shall affix the notary's official seal near the notary's official signature on the notarial certificate of a record.

(b) A notary's official seal shall include all of the following elements:

(1) The notary's name exactly as commissioned.

(2) The words "Notary Public".

(3) The county of commissioning, including the word "County" or the abbreviation "Co.".

(4) The words "North Carolina" or the abbreviation "N.C." or "NC".

(c) The notary seal may be either circular or rectangular in shape. Upon receiving a commission or a recommission on or after October 1, 2006, a notary shall not use a circular seal that is less than 1 1/2 inches, nor more than 2 inches in diameter. The rectangular seal shall not be over 1 inch high and 2 1/2 inches long. The perimeter of the seal shall contain a border that is visible when impressed.

(c1) Alterations to any information contained within the seal as embossed or stamped on the record are prohibited.

(d) A notarial seal, as it appears on a record, may contain the permanently imprinted, handwritten, or typed date the notary's commission expires.

(e) Any reference in the General Statutes to the seal of a notary shall include the stamp of a notary, and any reference to the stamp of a notary shall include the seal of the notary.

(f) The failure of a notarial seal to comply with the requirements of this section shall not affect the sufficiency, validity, or enforceability of the notarial certificate, but shall constitute a violation of the notary's duties. (2005-391, s. 4; 2006-59, s. 17; 2013-204, s. 1.2.)

§ 10B-38: Reserved for future codification purposes.

§ 10B-39: Reserved for future codification purposes.

Part 6. Certificate Forms.

§ 10B-40. Notarial certificates in general.

(a) A notary shall not make or give a notarial certificate unless the notary has either personal knowledge or satisfactory evidence of the identity of the principal or, if applicable, the subscribing witness.

(a1) By making or giving a notarial certificate, whether or not stated in the certificate, a notary certifies as follows:

(1) As to an acknowledgment, all those things described in G.S. 10B-3(1).

(2) As to an affirmation, all those things described in G.S. 10B-3(2).

(3) As to an oath, all those things described in G.S. 10B-3(14).

(4) As to a verification or proof, all those things described in G.S. 10B-3(28).

(a2) In addition to the certifications under subsection (a1) of this section, by making or giving a notarial certificate, whether or not stated in the certificate, a notary certifies to all of the following:

(1) At the time the notarial act was performed and the notarial certificate was signed by the notary, the notary was lawfully commissioned, the notary's commission had neither expired nor been suspended, the notarial act was

performed within the geographic limits of the notary's commission, and the notarial act was performed in accordance with the provision of this Chapter.

(2)   If the notarial certificate is for an acknowledgment or the administration of an oath or affirmation, the person whose signature was notarized did not appear in the judgment of the notary to be incompetent, lacking in understanding of the nature and consequences of the transaction requiring the notarial act, or acting involuntarily, under duress, or undue influence.

(3)   The notary was not prohibited from acting under G.S. 10-20(c).

(a3)   The inclusion of additional information in a notarial certificate, including the representative or fiduciary capacity in which a person signed or the means a notary used to identify a principal, shall not invalidate an otherwise sufficient notarial certificate.

(b)   A notarial certificate for the acknowledgment taken by a notary of a principal who is an individual acting in his or her own right or who is an individual acting in a representative or fiduciary capacity is sufficient and shall be accepted in this State if it is substantially in the form set forth in G.S. 10B-41, if it is substantially in a form otherwise prescribed by the laws of this State, or if it includes all of the following:

(1)   Identifies the state and county in which the acknowledgment occurred.

(2)   Names the principal who appeared in person before the notary.

(3)   Repealed by Session Laws 2006-59, s. 18, effective October 1, 2006, and except as otherwise set forth in the act, applicable to notarial acts performed on or after October 1, 2006.

(4)   Indicates that the principal appeared in person before the notary and the principal acknowledged that he or she signed the record.

(5)   States the date of the acknowledgment.

(6)   Contains the signature and seal or stamp of the notary who took the acknowledgment.

(7)   States the notary's commission expiration date.

(c) A notarial certificate for the verification or proof of the signature of a principal by a subscribing witness taken by a notary is sufficient and shall be accepted in this State if it is substantially in the form set forth in G.S. 10B-42, if it is substantially in a form otherwise prescribed by the laws of this State, or if it includes all of the following:

(1) Identifies the state and county in which the verification or proof occurred.

(2) Names the subscribing witness who appeared in person before the notary.

(3) Repealed by Session Laws 2006-59, s. 18, effective October 1, 2006.

(4) Names the principal whose signature on the record is to be verified or proven.

(5) Indicates that the subscribing witness certified to the notary under oath or by affirmation that the subscribing witness is not a party to or beneficiary of the transaction, signed the record as a subscribing witness, and either (i) witnessed the principal sign the record, or (ii) witnessed the principal acknowledge the principal's signature on the record.

(6) States the date of the verification or proof.

(7) Contains the signature and seal or stamp of the notary who took the verification or proof.

(8) States the notary's commission expiration date.

(c1) A notarial certificate for the verification or proof of the signature of a principal or a subscribing witness by a nonsubscribing witness taken by a notary is sufficient and shall be accepted in this State if it is substantially in the form set forth in G.S. 10B-42.1, if it is substantially in a form otherwise prescribed by the laws of this State, or if it includes all of the following:

(1) Identifies the state and county in which the verification or proof occurred.

(2) Names the nonsubscribing witness who appeared in person before the notary.

(3) Names the principal or subscribing witness whose signature on the record is to be verified or proven.

(4) Indicates that the nonsubscribing witness certified to the notary under oath or by affirmation that the nonsubscribing witness is not a party to or beneficiary of the transaction and that the nonsubscribing witness recognizes the signature of either the principal or the subscribing witness and that the signature is genuine.

(5) States the date of the verification or proof.

(6) Contains the signature and seal or stamp of the notary who took the verification or proof.

(7) States the notary's commission expiration date.

(d) A notarial certificate for an oath or affirmation taken by a notary is sufficient and shall be accepted in this State if it is substantially in the form set forth in G.S. 10B-43, if it is substantially in a form otherwise prescribed by the laws of this State, or if it includes all of the following:

(1) Repealed by Session Laws 2006-59, s. 18, effective October 1, 2006.

(2) Names the principal who appeared in person before the notary unless the name of the principal otherwise is clear from the record itself.

(3) Repealed by Session Laws 2006-59, s. 18, effective October 1, 2006.

(4) Indicates that the principal who appeared in person before the notary signed the record in question and certified to the notary under oath or by affirmation as to the truth of the matters stated in the record.

(5) States the date of the oath or affirmation.

(6) Contains the signature and seal or stamp of the notary who took the oath or affirmation.

(7) States the notary's commission expiration date.

(e) Any notarial certificate made in another jurisdiction shall be sufficient in this State if it is made in accordance with federal law or the laws of the jurisdiction where the notarial certificate is made.

(f) On records to be filed, registered, recorded, or delivered in another state or jurisdiction of the United States, a North Carolina notary may complete any notarial certificate that may be required in that other state or jurisdiction.

(g) Nothing in this Chapter shall be deemed to authorize the use of a notarial certificate authorized by this Part in place of or as an alternative to a notarial certificate required by any other provision of the General Statutes outside of Chapter 47 of the General Statutes that prescribes the specific form or content for a notarial certificate including G.S. 31-11.6, Chapter 32A of the General Statutes, and G.S. 90-321. However, any statute that permits or requires the use of a notarial certificate contained within Chapter 47 of the General Statutes may also be satisfied by the use of a notarial certificate permitted by this Part. Any form of acknowledgment or probate authorized under Chapter 47 of the General Statutes shall be conclusively deemed in compliance with the requirements of this section.

(h) If an individual signs a record and purports to be acting in a representative or fiduciary capacity, that individual is also deemed to represent to the notary that he or she is signing the record with proper authority to do so and also is signing the record on behalf of the person or entity represented and identified therein or in the fiduciary capacity indicated therein. In performing a notarial act in relation to an individual described under this subsection, a notary is under no duty to verify whether the individual acted in a representative or fiduciary capacity or, if so, whether the individual was duly authorized so to do. A notarial certificate may include any of the following:

(1) A statement that an individual signed a record in a particular representative or fiduciary capacity.

(2) A statement that the individual who signed the record in a representative or fiduciary capacity had due authority so to do.

(3) A statement identifying the represented person or entity or the fiduciary capacity. (2005-391, s. 4; 2006-59, s. 18.)

§ 10B-41. Notarial certificate for an acknowledgment.

(a) When properly completed by a notary, a notarial certificate that substantially complies with the following form may be used and shall be sufficient under the law of this State to satisfy the requirements for a notarial certificate for the acknowledgment of a principal who is an individual acting in his or her own right or who is an individual acting in a representative or fiduciary capacity. The authorization of the form in this section does not preclude the use of other forms.

_____ County, North Carolina

I certify that the following person(s) personally appeared before me this day, each acknowledging to me that he or she signed the foregoing document: name(s) of principal(s).

Date: _____   Official Signature of Notary

                              Notary's printed or typed name,
Notary Public

    (Official Seal)   My commission expires:
_____

(b) Repealed by Session Laws 2006-59, s. 19, effective October 1, 2006, and except as otherwise set forth in the act, applicable to notarial acts performed on or after October 1, 2006.

(c) The notary's printed or typed name as shown in the form provided in subsection (a) of this section is not required if the legible appearance of the notary's name may be ascertained from the notary's typed or printed name near the notary's signature or from elsewhere in the notarial certificate or from the notary's seal if the name is legible. (2005-391, s. 4; 2006-59, s. 19.)

§ 10B-42. Notarial certificate for a verification or of subscribing witness.

(a) When properly completed by a notary, a notarial certificate in substantially the following form may be used and shall be sufficient under the law of this State to satisfy the requirements for a notarial certificate for the verification or proof of the signature of a principal by a subscribing witness. The authorization of the form in this section does not preclude the use of other forms.

_____ County, North Carolina

I certify that (name of subscribing witness) personally appeared before me this day and certified to me under oath or by affirmation that he or she is not a grantee or beneficiary of the transaction, signed the foregoing document as a subscribing witness, and either (i) witnessed (name of principal) sign the foregoing document or (ii) witnessed (name of principal) acknowledge his or her signature on the already-signed document.

Date: _____   Official Signature of Notary

Notary's printed or typed name,
Notary Public

(Official Seal)   My commission expires: _____

(b) Repealed by Session Laws 2006-59, s. 20, effective October 1, 2006, except as otherwise set forth in the act, and applicable to notarial acts performed on or after October 1, 2006.

(c) The notary's printed or typed name as shown in the form provided in subsection (a) of this section is not required if the legible appearance of the notary's name may be ascertained from the notary's typed or printed name near the notary's signature or from elsewhere in the notarial certificate or from the notary's seal if the name is legible. (2005-391, s. 4; 2006-59, s. 20.)

§ 10B-42.1. Notarial certificate for a verification of nonsubscribing witness.

(a) When properly completed by a notary, a notarial certificate in substantially the following form may be used and shall be sufficient under the law of this State to satisfy the requirements for a notarial certificate for the verification or proof of the signature of a principal or subscribing witness by a nonsubscribing witness. The authorization of the form in this section does not preclude the use of other forms.

_____ County, North Carolina

I certify (name of nonsubscribing witness) personally appeared before me this day and certified to me under oath or by affirmation that he or she is not a grantee or beneficiary of the transaction, that (name of nonsubscribing witness) recognizes the signature of (name of the principal or the subscribing witness) and that the signature is genuine.

Date: _____   Official Signature of Notary

                                                Notary's printed or typed name,
Notary Public

       (Official Seal)   My commission expires:

_____

(b)   The notary's printed or typed name as shown in the form provided in subsection (a) of this section is not required if the legible appearance of the notary's name may be ascertained from the notary's typed or printed name near the notary's signature or from elsewhere in the notarial certificate or from the notary's seal if the name is legible. (2006-59, s. 21.)

§ 10B-43. Notarial certificate for an oath or affirmation.

(a)   When properly completed by a notary, a notarial certificate that substantially complies with either of the following forms may be used and shall be sufficient under the law of this State to satisfy the requirements for a notarial certificate for an oath or affirmation. The authorization of the forms in this section does not preclude the use of other forms.

_____ County, North Carolina

Signed and sworn to before me this day by (name of principal).

Date: _____   Official Signature of Notary

                                                Notary's printed or typed name,
Notary Public

(Official Seal)   My commission expires:

_____

-OR-

_____ County, North Carolina

Sworn to and subscribed before me this day by (name of principal).

Date: _____   Official Signature of Notary

                                              Notary's printed or typed name,
Notary Public

(Official Seal)   My commission expires:

_____

(b)   Repealed by Session Laws 2006-59, s. 22, effective October 1, 2006, except as otherwise set forth in the act, and applicable to notarial acts performed on or after October 1, 2006.

(c)   The notary's printed or typed name as shown in the form provided in subsection (a) of this section is not required if the legible appearance of the notary's name may be ascertained from the notary's typed or printed name near the notary's signature or from elsewhere in the notarial certificate or from the notary's seal if the name is legible.

(d)   In either of the forms provided under subsection (a) of this section all of the following shall apply:

(1)   The name of the principal may be omitted if the name of the principal is located near the jurat, and the principal who so appeared before the notary is clear from the record itself.

(2)   The words "affirmed" or "sworn to or affirmed" may be substituted for the words "sworn to". (2005-391, s. 4; 2006-59, s. 22.)

§ 10B-44: Reserved for future codification purposes.

§ 10B-45: Reserved for future codification purposes.

§ 10B-46: Reserved for future codification purposes.

§ 10B-47: Reserved for future codification purposes.

§ 10B-48: Reserved for future codification purposes.

§ 10B-49: Reserved for future codification purposes.

Part 7. Changes in Status.

§ 10B-50. Change of address.

Within 45 days after the change of a notary's residence, business, or any mailing address or telephone number, the notary shall send to the Secretary by fax, e-mail, or certified mail, return receipt requested, a signed notice of the change, giving both old and new addresses or telephone numbers. (1991, c. 683, s. 2; 1995, c. 226, s. 3; 2005-391, s. 4.)

§ 10B-51. Change of name.

(a) Within 45 days after the legal change of a notary's name, the notary shall send to the Secretary by fax, e-mail, or certified mail, return receipt requested, a signed notice of the change. The notice shall include both the notary's former name and the notary's new name.

(b) A notary with a new name may continue to use the former name in performing notarial acts until all of the following steps have been completed:

(1) The notary receives a confirmation of Notary's Name Change from the Secretary.

(2) The notary obtains a new seal bearing the new name exactly as that name appears in the confirmation from the Secretary.

(3) The notary appears before the register of deeds to which the commission was delivered within 45 days of the effective date of the change to

be duly qualified by taking the general oath of office prescribed in G.S. 11-11 and the oath prescribed for officers in G.S. 11-7 under the new name and to have the notary public record changed to reflect the new commissioned name.

(c)   Upon completion of the requirements in subsection (b) of this section, the notary shall use the new name. (1991, c. 683, s. 2; 1995, c. 226, s. 3; 2005-391, s. 4.)

§ 10B-52. Change of county.

(a)   A notary who has moved to another county in North Carolina remains commissioned until the current commission expires, is not required to obtain a new seal, and may continue to notarize without changing his or her seal.

(b)   When a notary who has moved applies to be recommissioned, if the commission is granted the, Secretary shall issue a notice of recommissioning. The commission applicant shall then do all of the following:

(1)   Obtain a new seal bearing the new county exactly as in the notice of recommissioning.

(2)   Appear before the register of deeds to which the commission was delivered within 45 days of recommissioning, to be duly qualified by taking the general oath of office prescribed in G.S. 11-11 and the oath prescribed for officers in G.S. 11-7 under the new county and to have the notary public record changed to reflect the new county name. (1991, c. 683, s. 2; 1995, c. 226; s. 3; 2005-391, s. 4.)

§ 10B-53. Change of both name and county.

Within 45 days after the legal change of a notary's name, and if the notary has also moved to a different county than as last commissioned, the notary shall submit to the Secretary a recommissioning application and fee pursuant to this Chapter. The notary may continue to perform notarial acts under the notary's previous name and seal until all of the following steps have been completed:

(1)   The notary receives a transmittal receipt of reappointment due to name and county change from the Secretary.

(2)   The notary obtains a new seal bearing the new name and county exactly as those items appear in the transmittal receipt.

(3)   The notary appears before the register of deeds to which the commission was delivered within 45 days of recommissioning to be duly qualified by taking the general oath of office prescribed in G.S. 11-11 and the oath prescribed for officers in G.S. 11-7 under the new name and county and to have the notary public record changed to reflect the new name and county. (1991, c. 683, s. 2; 1995, c. 226, s. 3; 2005-391, s. 4.)

§ 10B-54. Resignation.

(a)   A notary who resigns the notary's commission shall send to the Secretary by fax, e-mail, or certified mail, return receipt requested, a signed notice indicating the effective date of resignation.

(b)   Notaries who cease to reside in or to maintain a regular place of work or business in this State, or who become permanently unable to perform their notarial duties, shall resign their commissions and shall deliver their seals to the Secretary by certified mail, return receipt requested. (2005-391, s. 4.)

§ 10B-55. Disposition of seal; death of notary.

(a)   When a notary commission is resigned or revoked, the notary shall deliver the notary's seal to the Secretary within 45 days of the resignation or revocation. Delivery shall be accomplished by certified mail, return receipt requested. The Secretary shall destroy any seal received under this subsection.

(b)   A notary whose commission has expired and whose previous commission or application was not revoked or denied by this State, is not required to deliver the seal to the Secretary as provided under subsection (a) of this section if the notary intends to apply to be recommissioned and is recommissioned within three months after the notary's commission expires.

(c)   If a notary dies while commissioned or before fulfilling the disposition of seal requirements in this section, the notary's estate shall, as soon as is reasonably practicable and no later than the closing of the estate, notify the Secretary in writing of the notary's death and deliver the notary's seal to the Secretary for destruction. A personal representative who is not a notary does not have to comply with the provisions of this subsection if he or she provides a statement under oath in any enforcement proceeding that he or she was unaware that the decedent was a commissioned notary public at the time of death. (2005-391, s. 4; 2013-204, s. 1.3.)

§ 10B-56: Reserved for future codification purposes.

§ 10B-57: Reserved for future codification purposes.

§ 10B-58: Reserved for future codification purposes.

§ 10B-59: Reserved for future codification purposes.

Part 8. Enforcement, Sanctions, and Remedies.

§ 10B-60. Enforcement and penalties.

(a) The Secretary may issue a warning to a notary or restrict, suspend, or revoke a notarial commission for a violation of this Chapter and on any ground for which an application for a commission may be denied under this Chapter. Any period of restriction, suspension, or revocation shall not extend the expiration date of a commission.

(b) Except as otherwise permitted by law, a person who commits any of the following acts is guilty of a Class 1 misdemeanor:

(1) Holding one's self out to the public as a notary if the person does not have a commission.

(2) Performing a notarial act if the person's commission has expired or been suspended or restricted.

(3) Performing a notarial act before the person had taken the oath of office.

(c) A notary shall be guilty of a Class 1 misdemeanor if the notary does any of the following:

(1) Takes an acknowledgment or administers an oath or affirmation without the principal appearing in person before the notary.

(2) Takes a verification or proof without the subscribing witness appearing in person before the notary.

(3) Takes an acknowledgment or administers an oath or affirmation without personal knowledge or satisfactory evidence of the identity of the principal.

(4) Takes a verification or proof without personal knowledge or satisfactory evidence of the identity of the subscribing witness.

(d) A notary shall be guilty of a Class I felony if the notary does any of the following:

(1) Takes an acknowledgment or a verification or a proof, or administers an oath or affirmation if the notary knows it is false or fraudulent.

(2) Takes an acknowledgment or administers an oath or affirmation without the principal appearing in person before the notary if the notary does so with the intent to commit fraud.

(3) Takes a verification or proof without the subscribing witness appearing in person before the notary if the notary does so with the intent to commit fraud.

(e) It is a Class I felony for any person to perform notarial acts in this State with the knowledge that the person is not commissioned under this Chapter.

(f) Any person who without authority obtains, uses, conceals, defaces, or destroys the seal or notarial records of a notary is guilty of a Class I felony.

(g) For purposes of enforcing this Chapter and Article 34 of Chapter 66 of the General Statutes, the following provisions are applicable:

(1) Law enforcement agents of the Department of the Secretary of State have statewide jurisdiction and have all of the powers and authority of law enforcement officers. The agents have the authority to assist local law enforcement agencies in their investigations and to initiate and carry out, on their own or in coordination with local law enforcement agencies, investigations of violations.

(2) Any party to a transaction requiring a notarial certificate for verification and any attorney licensed in this State who is involved in such a transaction in

any capacity, whether or not the attorney is representing one of the parties to the transaction, may execute an affidavit and file it with the Secretary of State, setting forth the actions which the affiant alleges constitute violations. Upon receipt of the affidavit, law enforcement agents of the Department shall initiate and carry out, on their own or in coordination with local law enforcement agencies, investigations of violations.

(h) Resignation or expiration of a notarial commission does not terminate or preclude an investigation into a notary's conduct by the Secretary, who may pursue the investigation to a conclusion, whereupon it may be a matter of public record whether or not the finding would have been grounds for disciplinary action.

(i) The Secretary may seek injunctive relief against any person who violates the provisions of this Chapter. Nothing in this Chapter diminishes the authority of the North Carolina State Bar.

(j) Any person who knowingly solicits, coerces, or in any material way influences a notary to commit official misconduct, is guilty as an aider and abettor and is subject to the same level of punishment as the notary.

(k) The sanctions and remedies of this Chapter supplement other sanctions and remedies provided by law, including, but not limited to, forgery and aiding and abetting.

(l) The Secretary shall notify the North Carolina State Bar (State Bar) of any final decision finding a violation of subsection (a) of this section by a notary who is also an attorney-at-law licensed under Chapter 84 of the General Statutes. The Secretary shall endeavor to provide a copy of any court order rendered under subsection (b), (c), (d), (e), (f), or (j) of this section to the State Bar in cases where the notary is an attorney-at-law licensed under Chapter 84 of the General Statutes. Any referral by the Secretary to the State Bar under this subsection shall be considered a showing of professional unfitness under G.S. 84-28(d), and the State Bar shall administer discipline accordingly. (1991, c. 683, s. 2; 1993, c. 539, ss. 6-8, 1121; 1994 Ex. Sess., c. 24, s. 14(c); 1995, c. 226, s. 4; 2001-450, s. 3; 2005-391, s. 4; 2006-59, s. 23; 2013-204, s. 1.4; 2013-387, s. 5.)

§ 10B-61: Reserved for future codification purposes.

§ 10B-62: Reserved for future codification purposes.

§ 10B-63: Reserved for future codification purposes.

§ 10B-64: Reserved for future codification purposes.

Part 9. Validation of Notarial Acts.

§ 10B-65. Acts of notaries public in certain instances validated.

(a)   Any acknowledgment taken and any instrument notarized by a person prior to qualification as a notary public but after commissioning or recommissioning as a notary public, or by a person whose notary commission has expired, is hereby validated. The acknowledgment and instrument shall have the same legal effect as if the person qualified as a notary public at the time the person performed the act.

(b)   All documents bearing a notarial seal and which contain any of the following errors are validated and given the same legal effect as if the errors had not occurred:

(1)   The date of the expiration of the notary's commission is stated, whether correctly or erroneously.

(2)   The notarial seal does not contain a readable impression of the notary's name, contains an incorrect spelling of the notary's name, or does not bear the name of the notary exactly as it appears on the commission, as required under G.S. 10B-37.

(3)   The notary's signature does not comport exactly with the name on the notary commission or on the notary seal, as required by G.S. 10B-20.

(4)   The notarial seal contains typed, printed, drawn, or handwritten material added to the seal, fails to contain the words "North Carolina" or the abbreviation "NC", or contains correct information except that instead of the abbreviation for North Carolina contains the abbreviation for another state.

(5) The date of the acknowledgement, the verification or proof, or the oath or affirmation states the correct day and month but lacks a year or states an incorrect year.

(c) All deeds of trust in which the notary was named in the document as a trustee only are validated.

(d) All notary acknowledgments performed before December 1, 2005, bearing a notarial seal are hereby validated.

(e) This section applies to notarial acts performed on or before April 1, 2013. (1945, c. 665; 1947, c. 313; 1949, c. 1; 1953, c. 702; 1961, cc. 483, 734; 1965, c. 37; 1969, c. 83; c. 716, s. 1; 1971, c. 229, s. 1; 1973, c. 680, s. 1; 1977, c. 734, s. 1; 1979, c. 226, s. 2; c. 643, s. 1; 1981, c. 164, ss. 1, 2; 1983, c. 205, s. 1; 1985, c. 71, s. 1; 1987, c. 277, s. 9; 1989, c. 390, s. 9; 1991, c. 683, s. 2; 1997-19, s. 1; 1997-469, s. 2; 1998-228, s. 10; 1999-21, s. 2; 2001-154, s. 1; 2002-159, s. 27; 2003-38, s. 1; 2004-199, s. 6.; 2005-391, s. 4; 2008-194, s. 5; 2013-204, s. 1.5.)

§ 10B-66. Certain notarial acts validated.

(a) Any acknowledgment taken and any instrument notarized by a person whose notarial commission was revoked on or before January 30, 1997, is hereby validated.

(b) This section applies to notarial acts performed on or before August 1, 1998. (2005-391, s. 4.)

§ 10B-67. Erroneous commission expiration date cured.

An erroneous statement of the date that the notary's commission expires shall not affect the sufficiency, validity, or enforceability of the notarial certificate or the related record if the notary is, in fact, lawfully commissioned at the time of the notarial act. This section applies to notarial acts whenever performed. (2006-59, s. 24; 2013-204, s. 1.6.)

§ 10B-68. Technical defects cured.

(a) Technical defects, errors, or omissions in a notarial certificate shall not affect the sufficiency, validity, or enforceability of the notarial certificate or the related instrument or document.

(b) Defects in the commissioning or recommissioning of a notary that are approved by the Department are cured. This subsection applies to commissions and recommissions issued on or after December 1, 2005.

(c) As used in this section, a technical defect includes those cured under G.S. 10B-37(f) and G.S. 10B-67. Other technical defects include, but are not limited to, the absence of the legible appearance of the notary's name exactly as shown on the notary's commission as required in G.S. 10B-20(b), the affixation of the notary's seal near the signature of the principal or subscribing witness rather than near the notary's signature, minor typographical mistakes in the spelling of the principal's name, the failure to acknowledge the principal's name exactly as signed by including or omitting initials, or the failure to specify the principal's title or office, if any. (2006-59, s. 24; 2006-199, s. 2; 2013-204, s. 1.7.)

§ 10B-69. Official forms cured.

(a) The notarial certificate contained in a form issued by a State agency prior to April 1, 2013, is deemed to be a valid certificate provided the certificate complied with the law at the time the form was issued.

(b) The notarization using a certificate under subsection (a) of this section shall be deemed valid if executed in compliance with the law at the time the form was issued. (2006-59, s. 24; 2013-204, s. 1.8.)

§ 10B-70. Certain notarial acts for local government agencies validated.

(a) Any acknowledgment taken and any instrument notarized for a local government agency by a person prior to qualification as a notary public but after commissioning or recommissioning as a notary public, by a person whose notary commission has expired, or by a person who failed to qualify within 45 days of commissioning as required by G.S. 10B-10, is hereby validated. The acknowledgment and instrument shall have the same legal effect as if the person qualified as a notary public at the time the person performed the act.

This section shall apply to notarial acts performed for a local government agency on or after October 31, 2006, and before June 30, 2007.

(b)   Any electronic document filed in the Mecklenburg County Register of Deeds office that purports to be notarized in the Commonwealth of Virginia and that contains the typed name of a Virginia notary together with the notary's expiration date shall be given the same legal effect as if the person performed a lawful notarization in Virginia. (2007-484, s. 27; 2008-194, s. 4.)

§ 10B-71. Certain notarial acts validated when recommissioned notary failed to again take oath.

Any acknowledgment taken and any instrument notarized by a person who after recommissioning failed to again take the oath as a notary public is hereby validated. The acknowledgment and instrument shall have the same legal effect as if the person qualified as a notary public at the time the person performed the act. This section shall apply to notarial acts performed on or after May 15, 2004, and before April 1, 2013. (2009-358, s. 1; 2013-204, s. 1.9.)

§ 10B-72. Certain notarial acts validated when recommissioned notary failed to again take oath.

Any acknowledgment taken and any instrument notarized by a person who after recommissioning failed to again take the oath as a notary public is hereby validated. The acknowledgment and instrument shall have the same legal effect as if the person qualified as a notary public at the time the person performed the act. This section shall apply to notarial acts performed on or after August 28, 2010, and before January 12, 2012. (2012-194, s. 65.)

§ 10B-73. Reserved for future codification purposes.

§ 10B-74. Reserved for future codification purposes.

§ 10B-75. Reserved for future codification purposes.

§ 10B-76. Reserved for future codification purposes.

§ 10B-77. Reserved for future codification purposes.

§ 10B-78. Reserved for future codification purposes.

§ 10B-79. Reserved for future codification purposes.

§ 10B-80. Reserved for future codification purposes.

§ 10B-81. Reserved for future codification purposes.

§ 10B-82. Reserved for future codification purposes.

§ 10B-83. Reserved for future codification purposes.

§ 10B-84. Reserved for future codification purposes.

§ 10B-85. Reserved for future codification purposes.

§ 10B-86. Reserved for future codification purposes.

§ 10B-87. Reserved for future codification purposes.

§ 10B-88. Reserved for future codification purposes.

§ 10B-89. Reserved for future codification purposes.

§ 10B-90. Reserved for future codification purposes.

§ 10B-91. Reserved for future codification purposes.

§ 10B-92. Reserved for future codification purposes.

§ 10B-93. Reserved for future codification purposes.

§ 10B-94. Reserved for future codification purposes.

§ 10B-95. Reserved for future codification purposes.

§ 10B-96. Reserved for future codification purposes.

§ 10B-97. Reserved for future codification purposes.

§ 10B-98. Reserved for future codification purposes.

§ 10B-99. Presumption of regularity.

(a) In the absence of evidence of fraud on the part of the notary, or evidence of a knowing and deliberate violation of this Article by the notary, the courts shall grant a presumption of regularity to notarial acts so that those acts may be upheld, provided there has been substantial compliance with the law. Nothing in this Chapter modifies or repeals the common law doctrine of substantial compliance in effect on November 30, 2005.

(b) A notarial act shall be deemed valid if it complies with the law as it existed on or before December 1, 2005. This section applies to notarial acts whenever performed. (2006-59, s. 24; 2006-199, s. 4; 2013-204, s. 1.10.)

Article 2.

Electronic Notary Act.

Part 1. General Provisions.

§ 10B-100. Short title.

This Article Is the Electronic Notary Public Act and may be cited by that name. (2005-391, s. 4.)

§ 10B-101. Definitions.

The following definitions apply in this Article:

(1) "Electronic" means relating to technology having electrical, digital, magnetic, wireless, optical, electromagnetic, or similar capabilities.

(2) "Electronic Document" means information that is created, generated, sent, communicated, received, or stored by electronic means.

(3) "Electronic Notarial Act" and "Electronic Notarization" mean an official act by an electronic notary public that involves electronic documents.

(4) "Electronic Notary Public" and "Electronic Notary" mean a notary public who has registered with the Secretary the capability of performing electronic notarial acts in conformance with this Article.

(5) "Electronic Notary Seal" and "Electronic Seal" mean information within a notarized electronic document that includes the notary's name, jurisdiction, and commission expiration date, and generally corresponds to data in notary seals used on paper documents.

(6) "Electronic Signatures" means an electronic symbol or process attached to or logically associated with an electronic document and executed or adopted by a person with the intent to sign the document.

(7) "Notary's Electronic Signature" means those forms of electronic signature which have been approved by the Secretary as authorized in G.S. 10B-125, as an acceptable means for an electronic notary to affix the notary's official signature to an electronic record that is being notarized. (2005-391, s. 4.)

§ 10B-102. Scope of this Article.

Article 1 of this Chapter applies to all acts authorized under this Article unless the provisions of Article 1 directly conflict with the provisions of this Article, in which case provisions of Article 2 shall control. (2005-391, s. 4.)

§ 10B-103. Reserved for future codification purposes.

§ 10B-104. Reserved for future codification purposes.

Part 2. Registration.

§ 10B-105. Qualifications.

(a) A person qualified for electronic notary registration shall meet all of the following requirements:

(1) Hold a valid commission as a notary public in the State of North Carolina.

(2) Except as otherwise provided, abide by all the provisions of Article 1 of this Chapter.

(3) Satisfy the requirements of G.S. 10B-107.

(4) Submit an electronic registration form containing no significant misstatement or omission of fact.

(b) The Secretary may deny a registration as an electronic notary as authorized in G.S. 10B-5(d). (2005-391, s. 4.)

§ 10B-106. Registration with the Secretary of State.

(a) Before performing notarial acts electronically, a notary shall register the capability to notarize electronically with the Secretary.

(b) The term of registration as an electronic notary shall coincide with the term of the notary's commission under Article 1 of this Chapter.

(c) An electronic notary shall reregister the capability to notarize electronically at the same time the notary applies for recommissioning under the requirements of Article 1 of this Chapter.

(d) An electronic form shall be used by an electronic notary in registering with the Secretary and it shall include, at least all of the following:

(1) The applicant's full legal name and the name to be used for commissioning, excluding nicknames.

(2) The state and county of commissioning of the registrant.

(3) The expiration date of the registrant's notary commission.

(4) Proof of successful completion of the course of instruction on electronic notarization as required by this Article.

(5)   A description of the technology the registrant will use to create an electronic signature in performing official acts.

(6)   If the device used to create the registrant's electronic signature was issued or registered through a licensed certification authority, the name of that authority, the source of the license, the starting and expiration dates of the device's term of registration, and any revocations, annulments, or other premature terminations of any registered device of the registrant that was due to misuse or compromise of the device, with the date, cause, and nature of each termination explained in detail.

(7)   The e-mail address of the registrant.

The information provided in a registration that relates to subdivision (7) of this section shall be considered confidential information and shall not be subject to disclosure under Chapter 132 of the General Statutes, except as provided by rule.

(e)   The electronic registration form for an electronic notary shall be transmitted electronically to the Secretary and shall include any decrypting instructions, codes, keys, or software that allow the registration to be read.

(f)   Within 10 business days after the change of any registration information required of an electronic notary, the notary shall electronically transmit to the Secretary a notice of the change of information signed with the notary's official electronic signature. (2005-391, s. 4; 2006-59, s. 25; 2006-259, ss. 1, 3.)

§ 10B-107. Course of instruction.

(a)   Before performing electronic notarial acts, a notary shall take a course of instruction of least three hours approved by the Secretary and pass an examination of this course, which shall be in addition to the educational requirements provided in Article 1 of this Chapter.

(b)   The content of the course and the basis for the examination shall be notarial laws, procedures, technology, and ethics as they pertain to electronic notarization. (2005-391, s. 4.)

§ 10B-108. Fees for registration.

The fee payable to the Secretary for registering or reregistering as an electronic notary is fifty dollars ($50.00), which shall be in addition to the fee required in G.S. 10B-13. All funds received by the Secretary under this section shall be deposited into the General Fund. (2005-391, s. 4.)

§ 10B-109: Reserved for future codification purposes.

§ 10B-110: Reserved for future codification purposes.

§ 10B-111: Reserved for future codification purposes.

§ 10B-112: Reserved for future codification purposes.

§ 10B-113: Reserved for future codification purposes.

§ 10B-114: Reserved for future codification purposes.

Part 3. Electronic Notarial Acts, Powers, and Limitations.

§ 10B-115. Types of electronic notarial acts.

The following types of notarial acts may be performed electronically:

(1)   Acknowledgments;

(2)   Jurats;

(3)   Verifications or proofs; and

(4)   Oaths or affirmations. (2005-391, s. 4.)

§ 10B-116. Prohibitions.

An electronic notarization shall not be performed if the signer of the electronic document:

(1) Is not in the presence of the electronic notary at the time of notarization; and

(2) Is not personally known to the notary or identified by the evidence in accordance with other provisions of this Chapter; or

(3) For any reason set forth in G.S. 10B-20. (2005-391, s. 4.)

§ 10B-117. Notarial components of electronic document.

In performing an electronic notarial act, all of the following components shall be attached to, or logically associated with, the electronic document by the electronic notary, all of which shall be immediately perceptible and reproducible in the electronic record to which the notary's electronic signature is attached:

(1) The notary's name, state, and county of commissioning exactly as stated on the commission issued by the Secretary;

(2) The words "Electronic Notary Public";

(3) The words "State of North Carolina";

(4) The expiration date of the commission;

(5) The notary's electronic signature; and

(6) The completed wording of one of the following notarial certificates:

a. Acknowledgment;

b. Jurat;

c. Verification or proof; or

d. Oath or affirmation. (2005-391, s. 4.)

§ 10B-118. Maximum fees.

For performing electronic notarial acts, the maximum fees that may be charged by an electronic notary are as follows:

(1) For acknowledgments, $10.00 per signature.

(2) For jurats, $10.00 per signature.

(3) For verifications or proofs, $10.00 per signature.

(4) For oaths or affirmations, $10.00 per signature. (2005-391, s. 4.)

§ 10B-119: Reserved for future codification purposes.

§ 10B-120: Reserved for future codification purposes.

§ 10B-121: Reserved for future codification purposes.

§ 10B-122: Reserved for future codification purposes.

§ 10B-123: Reserved for future codification purposes.

§ 10B-124: Reserved for future codification purposes.

Part 4. Electronic Notary Records, Maintenance, and Disposition.

§ 10B-125. Electronic signature, electronic seal.

(a) The notary's electronic signature in combination with the electronic notary seal shall be used only for the purpose of performing electronic notarial acts.

(b) The Secretary shall adopt rules necessary to establish standards, procedures, practices, forms, and records relating to a notary's electronic signature and electronic seal. The notary's electronic seal and electronic signature shall conform to any standards adopted by the Secretary. (2005-391, s. 4.)

§ 10B-126. Security measures.

(a)   A notary shall safeguard the notary's electronic signature, the notary's electronic seal, and all other notarial records. Notarial records shall be maintained by the notary, and the notary shall not surrender or destroy the records except as required by a court order or as allowed under rules adopted by the Secretary.

(b)   When not in use, the notary shall keep the notary's electronic signature, electronic seal, and all other notarial records secure, under the exclusive control of the notary, and shall not allow them to be used by any other notary or any other person.

(c)   A notary shall do the following within 10 days of discovering that the notary's electronic seal or electronic signature has been stolen, lost, damaged, or otherwise rendered incapable of affixing a legible image:

(1)   Inform the appropriate law enforcement agency in the case of theft or vandalism.

(2)   Notify the appropriate register of deeds and the Secretary in writing and signed in the official name in which he or she was commissioned.

(d)   The Secretary may adopt rules necessary to insure the integrity, security, and authenticity of electronic notarizations.

(e)   The Secretary may require an electronic notary to create and to maintain a record, journal, or entry of each electronic notarial act. The rule-making authority contained in this subsection shall become effective 18 months after December 1, 2005.

(f)   The failure of an electronic notary to produce within 10 days of the Department's request any record required by a rule adopted under this section shall result in the suspension of the electronic notary's power to act as a notary under the provision of this Chapter until the Secretary reinstates the notary's commission.

(g)   Upon resignation, revocation, or expiration of an electronic notary commission, or death of the notary, all notarial records required by statute or rule shall be delivered to the Secretary. (2005-391, s. 4.)

§ 10B-127. Maintenance of electronic device.

(a) An electronic notary shall take reasonable steps to ensure that any registered device used to create the notary's electronic signature is current and has not been revoked or terminated by its issuing or registering authority.

(b) If the registration of the device used to create electronic signatures either expires or is changed during the electronic notary's term of office, the notary shall cease performing electronic notarizations until:

(1) A new device is duly issued or registered to the notary; and

(2) An electronically signed notice is sent to the Secretary that shall include the starting and expiration dates of any new registration term and any other new information at variance with information in the most recently executed electronic registration form. (2005-391, s. 4.)

§ 10B-128. Disposition of records.

(a) Upon compliance with G.S. 10B-127 and except as provided in subsection (b) of this section, when an electronic notary's commission expires or is resigned or revoked, or when an electronic notary dies, the notary or the notary's duly authorized representative shall erase, delete, or destroy the coding, disk, certificate, card, software, file, or program that enables electronic affixation of the notary's official electronic signature.

(b) A former electronic notary whose previous commission or application was not revoked or denied by the Secretary need not erase, delete, or destroy the coding, disk, certificate, card, software, file, or program enabling electronic affixation of the official electronic signature if he or she is recommissioned and reregistered as an electronic notary using the same electronic signature within three months after commission expiration. (2005-391, s. 4.)

§ 10B-129: Reserved for future codification purposes.

§ 10B-130: Reserved for future codification purposes.

§ 10B-131: Reserved for future codification purposes.

§ 10B-132: Reserved for future codification purposes.

§ 10B-133: Reserved for future codification purposes.

§ 10B-134: Reserved for future codification purposes.

Part 5. Certificate Forms.

§ 10B-135. Validity of notarial certificates.

The provisions contained in Article 1, Part 6, of this Chapter, with regard to notarial certificate forms, are applicable for the purposes of this Article. (2005-391, s. 4.)

§ 10B-136. Form of evidence of authority of electronic notarial act.

Electronic evidence of the authenticity of the official electronic signature and electronic seal of an electronic notary of this State, if required, shall be attached to, or logically associated with, a notarized electronic document transmitted to another state or nation and shall be in the form of an electronic certificate of authority signed by the Secretary in conformance with any current and pertinent international treaties, agreements, and conventions subscribed to by the government of the United States. (2005-391, s. 4.)

§ 10B-137. Certificate of authority for electronic notarial act.

(a) An electronic certificate of authority evidencing the authenticity of the official electronic signature and electronic seal of an electronic notary of this State shall contain substantially the following words:

Certificate of Authority for an Electronic Notarial Act

I, _____ (name, title, jurisdiction of commissioning official) certify that _____ (name of electronic notary), the person named as an electronic notary public in the attached or associated document, was indeed registered as an electronic notary public for the State of North Carolina and authorized to act as such at the time of the document's electronic notarization.

To verify this Certificate of Authority for an Electronic Notarial Act, I have included herewith my electronic signature this _____ day of _____, 20__.

(Electronic signature (and seal) of commissioning official)

(b)   The Secretary may charge ten dollars ($10.00) for issuing an electronic certificate of authority. (2005-391, s. 4.)

§ 10B-138: Reserved for future codification purposes.

§ 10B-139: Reserved for future codification purposes.

§ 10B-140: Reserved for future codification purposes.

§ 10B-141: Reserved for future codification purposes.

§ 10B-142: Reserved for future codification purposes.

§ 10B-143: Reserved for future codification purposes.

§ 10B-144: Reserved for future codification purposes.

Part 6. Enforcement.

§ 10B-145. Restriction or revocation of registration.

The Secretary or the Secretary's designee shall have the authority to warn, restrict, suspend, or revoke an electronic notary registration for a violation of this Chapter and on any ground for which electronic notary registration may be denied under this Chapter. (2005-391, s. 4.)

§ 10B-146. Wrongful manufacture, distribution, or possession of software or hardware.

(a) Any person who knowingly creates, manufactures, or distributes software for the purpose of allowing a person to act as an electronic notary without being commissioned and registered in accordance with this act shall be guilty of a Class G felony.

(b) Any person who wrongfully obtains, conceals, damages, or destroys the certificate, disk, coding, card, program, software, file, or hardware enabling an electronic notary to affix an official electronic signature is guilty of a Class I felony. (2005-391, s. 4.)

Chapter 11.

Oaths.

Article 1.

General Provisions.

§ 11-1. Oaths and affirmations to be administered with solemnity.

Whereas, lawful oaths for discovery of truth and establishing right are necessary and highly conducive to the important end of good government; and being most solemn appeals to Almighty God, as the omniscient witness of truth and the just and omnipotent avenger of falsehood, and whereas, lawful affirmations for the discovery of truth and establishing right are necessary and highly conducive to the important end of good government, therefore, such oaths and affirmations ought to be taken and administered with the utmost solemnity. (1777, c. 108, s. 2, P.R.; R.C., c. 76, s. 1; Rev., s. 2353; C.S., s. 3188; 1985, c. 156, s. 1.)

§ 11-2. Administration of oaths.

Judges and other persons who may be empowered to administer oaths, shall (except in the cases in this Chapter excepted) require the party to be sworn to lay his hand upon the Holy Scriptures, in token of his engagement to speak the truth and in further token that, if he should swerve from the truth, he may be justly deprived of all the blessings of that holy book and made liable to that vengeance which he has imprecated on his own head. (1777, c. 108, s. 2, P.R.; R.C., c. 76, s. 1; Code, s. 3309; Rev., s. 2354; C.S., s. 3189; 1941, c. 11; 1971, c. 381, s. 9; 1985, c. 756, s. 2.)

§ 11-3. Administration of oath with uplifted hand.

When the person to be sworn shall be conscientiously scrupulous of taking a book oath in manner aforesaid, he shall be excused from laying hands upon, or touching the Holy Gospel; and the oath required shall be administered in the following manner, namely: He shall stand with his right hand lifted up towards heaven, in token of his solemn appeal to the Supreme God, and also in token that if he should swerve from the truth he would draw down the vengeance of heaven upon his head, and shall introduce the intended oath with these words, namely:

I, A.B., do appeal to God, as a witness of the truth and the avenger of falsehood, as I shall answer the same at the great day of judgment, when the secrets of all hearts shall be known (etc., as the words of the oath may be). (1777, c. 108, s. 3, P.R.; R.C., c. 76, s. 2; Code, s. 3310; Rev., s. 2355; C.S., s. 3190.)

§ 11-4. Affirmation in lieu of oath.

When a person to be sworn shall have conscientious scruples against taking an oath in the manner prescribed by G.S. 11-2, 11-3, or 11-7, he shall be permitted to be affirmed. In all cases the words of the affirmation shall be the same as the words of the prescribed oath, except that the word "affirm" shall be substituted for the word "swear" and the words "so help me God" shall be deleted. (1777, c. 108, s. 4, P.R.; c. 115, s. 42, P.R.; 1819, c. 1019, P.R.; 1821, c. 1112, P.R.; R.C., c. 76, s. 3; Code, s. 3311; Rev., s. 2356; C.S., s. 3191; 1985, c. 756, s. 3.)

§ 11-5. Oaths of corporations.

In all cases where a corporation is appointed administrator, executor, collector, or to any other fiduciary position, of which fiduciary an oath is required by law, such oath may be taken by such corporation by and through any officer or agent of said corporation who is authorized by law to verify pleadings in behalf of such corporation; and any oath so taken shall be valid as the oath of such corporation. Any oath heretofore taken in the manner aforesaid in behalf of a corporation as such fiduciary is hereby validated as the oath of such corporation. (1919, c. 89, ss. 1, 2; C.S., s. 3192.)

§ 11-6: Repealed by Session Laws 1985, c. 756, s. 4.

§ 11-7. Oath or affirmation to support Constitutions; all officers to take.

Every member of the General Assembly and every person elected or appointed to hold any office of trust or profit in the State shall, before taking office or entering upon the execution of the office, take and subscribe to the following oath:

"I, _____, do solemnly and sincerely swear that I will support the Constitution of the United States; that I will be faithful and bear true allegiance to the State of North Carolina, and to the constitutional powers and authorities which are or may be established for the government thereof; and that I will endeavor to support, maintain and defend the Constitution of said State, not inconsistent with the Constitution of the United States, to the best of my knowledge and ability; so help me God." (1781, c. 342, s. 1, P.R.; R.C., c. 76, s. 4; Code, s. 3312; Rev., s. 2358; C.S., s. 3194; 1985, c. 756, s. 5.)

§ 11-7.1. Who may administer oaths of office.

(a) Except as otherwise specifically required by statute, an oath of office may be administered by:

(1) A justice, judge, magistrate, clerk, assistant clerk, or deputy clerk of the General Court of Justice, a retired justice or judge of the General Court of Justice, or any member of the federal judiciary;

(2) The Secretary of State;

(3) A notary public;

(4) A register of deeds;

(5) A mayor of any city, town, or incorporated village;

(5a) A chairman of the board of commissioners of any county;

(6) A member of the House of Representatives or Senate of the General Assembly;

(7) The clerk of any county, city, town or incorporated village.

(b) The administration of an oath by any judge of the Court of Appeals prior to March 7, 1969, is hereby validated. (1953, c. 23; 1969, c. 44, s. 25; c. 499; c. 713, s. 1; 1971, c. 381, s. 10; 1977, c. 344, s. 2; 1979, c. 757; 1981, c. 682, s. 2; 1983, c. 648, s. 1; 1995, c. 147, s. 1.)

§ 11-8. When deputies may administer.

In all cases where any civil officer, in the discharge of his duties, is permitted by the law to administer an oath, the deputy of such officer, when discharging such duties, shall have authority to administer it, provided he is a sworn officer; and the oath thus administered by the deputy shall be as obligatory as if administered by the principal officer, and shall be attended with the same penalties in case of false swearing. (1836, c. 27, s. 2; R.C., c. 76, s. 7; Code, s. 3316; Rev., s. 2359; C.S., s. 3195.)

§ 11-9. Administration by certain officers.

The chairman of the board of county commissioners and the chairman of the board of education of the several counties may administer oaths in any matter or hearing before their respective boards. (1889, c. 529; 1899, c. 89; Rev., s. 2362; C.S., s. 3196.)

§ 11-10. When county surveyors may administer oaths.

The county surveyors of the several counties are empowered to administer oaths to all such persons as are required by law to be sworn in making partition of real estate, in establishing boundaries and in surveying vacant lands under warrants. (1881, c. 144; Code, s. 3314; Rev., s. 2361; C.S., s. 3197; 1959, c. 879, s. 4.)

Article 2.

Forms of Official and Other Oaths.

§ 11-11. Oaths of sundry persons; forms.

The oaths of office to be taken by the several persons hereafter named shall be in the words following the names of said persons respectively, in all cases after taking the separate oath required by Article VI, Section 7 of the Constitution of North Carolina:

Administrator

You swear (or affirm) that you believe A. B. died without leaving any last will and testament; that you will well and truly administer all and singular the goods and chattels, rights and credits of the said A. B., and a true and perfect inventory thereof return according to law; and that all other duties appertaining to the charge reposed in you, you will well and truly perform, according to law, and with your best skill and ability; so help you, God.

Attorney at Law

I, A. B., do swear (or affirm) that I will truly and honestly demean myself in the practice of an attorney, according to the best of my knowledge and ability; so help me, God.

Attorney General, State District Attorneys and County Attorneys

I, A. B., do solemnly swear (or affirm) that I will well and truly serve the State of North Carolina in the office of Attorney General (district attorney for the State or attorney for the State in the county of _____); I will, in the execution of my office, endeavor to have the criminal laws fairly and impartially administered, so far as in me lies, according to the best of my knowledge and ability; so help me, God.

Auditor

I, A. B., do solemnly swear (or affirm) that I will well and truly execute the trust reposed in me as auditor, without favor or partiality, according to law, to the best of my knowledge and ability; so help me, God.

Book Debt Oath

You swear (or affirm) that the matter in dispute is a book account; that you have no means to prove the delivery of such articles, as you propose to prove by your own oath, or any of them, but by yourself; and you further swear that the account rendered by you is just and true; and that you have given all just credits; so help you, God.

Book Debt Oath for Administrator

You, as executor or administrator of A. B., swear (or affirm) that you verily believe this account to be just and true, and that there are no witnesses, to your knowledge, capable of proving the delivery of the articles therein charged; and that you found the book or account so stated, and do not know of any other or further credit to be given than what is therein given; so help you, God.

Clerk of the Supreme Court

I, ____, do solemnly swear that I will discharge the duties of the office of clerk of the Supreme Court without prejudice, affection, favor, or partiality, according to law and to the best of my skill and ability, so help me, God.

Clerk of the Superior Court

I, A. B., do swear (or affirm) that, by myself or any other person, I neither have given, nor will I give, to any person whatsoever, any gratuity, fee, gift or reward, in consideration of my election or appointment to the office of clerk of the superior court for the county of ____; nor have I sold, or offered to sell, nor will I sell or offer to sell, my interest in the said office; I also solemnly swear that I do not, directly or indirectly, hold any other lucrative office in the State; and I do further swear that I will execute the office of clerk of the superior court for the county of ____ without prejudice, favor, affection or partiality, to the best of my skill and ability; so help me, God.

Commissioners Allotting a Year's Provisions

You and each of you swear (or affirm) that you will lay off and allot to the petitioner a year's provisions for herself and family, according to law, and with your best skill and ability; so help you, God.

Commissioners Dividing and Allotting Real Estate

You and each of you swear (or affirm) that, in the partition of the real estate now about to be made by you, you will do equal and impartial justice among the several claimants, according to their several rights, and agreeably to law; so help you, God.

Executor

You swear (or affirm) that you believe this writing to be and contain the last will and testament of A. B., deceased; and that you will well and truly execute the same by first paying debts and then devises, as far as the decedent's estate shall extend or the law shall charge you; and that you will well and faithfully execute the office of an executor, agreeably to the trust and confidence reposed in you, and according to law; so help you, God.

Grand Jury-Foreman of

You, as foreman of this grand inquest for the body of this county, shall diligently inquire and true presentment make of all such matters and things as shall be given you in charge; the State's counsel, your fellows' and your own you shall keep secret; you shall present no one for envy, hatred or malice; neither shall you leave anyone unpresented for fear, favor or affection, reward or the hope of reward; but you shall present all things truly, as they come to your knowledge, according to the best of your understanding; so help you, God.

Grand Jurors

The same oath which your foreman hath taken on his part, you and each of you shall well and truly observe and keep on your part; so help you, God.

Grand Jury-Officer of

You swear (or affirm) that you will faithfully carry all papers sent from the court to the grand jury, or from the grand jury to the court, without alteration or erasement, and without disclosing the contents thereof; so help you, God.

Jury-Officer of

You swear (or affirm) that you will keep every person sworn on this jury in some private and convenient place when in your charge. You shall not suffer any person to speak to them, neither shall you speak to them yourself, unless it be to ask them whether they are agreed in their verdict, but with leave of the court; so help you, God.

Oath for Petit Juror

You do solemnly swear (affirm) that you will truthfully and without prejudice or partiality try all issues in civil or criminal actions that come before you and give true verdicts according to the evidence, so help you, God.

Justice, Judge, or Magistrate of the General Court of Justice

I, ____, do solemnly swear (affirm) that I will administer justice without favoritism to anyone or to the State; that I will not knowingly take, directly or indirectly, any fee, gift, gratuity or reward whatsoever, for any matter or thing done by me or to be done by me by virtue of my office, except the salary and allowances by law provided; and that I will faithfully and impartially discharge all the duties of __ of the ____ Division of the General Court of Justice to the best of my ability and understanding, and consistent with the Constitution and laws of the State; so help me, God.

Register of Deeds

I, A. B., do solemnly swear (or affirm) that I will faithfully and truly, according to the best of my skill and ability, execute the duties of the office of register of deeds for the county of ____, in all things according to law; so help me, God.

Secretary of State

I, A. B., do swear (or affirm) that I will, in all respects, faithfully and honestly execute the office of Secretary of State of the State of North Carolina, during my continuance in office, according to law; so help me, God.

Sheriff

I, A. B., do solemnly swear (or affirm) that I will execute the office of sheriff of __ county to the best of my knowledge and ability, agreeably to law; and that I will not take, accept or receive, directly or indirectly, any fee, gift, bribe, gratuity or reward whatsoever, for returning any man to serve as a juror or for making any false return on any process to me directed; so help me, God.

Law Enforcement Officer

I, A. B., do solemnly swear (or affirm) that I will be alert and vigilant to enforce the criminal laws of this State; that I will not be influenced in any matter on account of personal bias or prejudice; that I will faithfully and impartially execute the duties of my office as a law enforcement officer according to the best of my skill, abilities, and judgment; so help me, God.

State Treasurer

I, A. B., do swear (or affirm) that, according to the best of my abilities and judgment, I will execute impartially the office of State Treasurer, in all things according to law, and account for the public taxes; and I will not, directly or indirectly, apply the public money to any other use than by law directed; so help me, God.

Surveyor for a County

I, A. B., do solemnly swear (or affirm) that I will well and impartially discharge the several duties of the office of surveyor for the county of ____, according to law; so help me, God.

Treasurer for a County

I, A. B., do solemnly swear (or affirm) that, according to the best of my skill and ability, I will execute impartially the office of treasurer for the county of ____, in all things according to law; that I will duly and faithfully account for all public moneys that may come into my hands, and will not, directly or indirectly, apply the same, or any part thereof, to any other use than by law directed; so help me, God.

Witness to Depose before the Grand Jury

You swear (or affirm) that the evidence you shall give to the grand jury, upon this bill of indictment against A. B., shall be the truth, the whole truth, and nothing but the truth; so help you, God.

Witness in a Capital Trial

You swear (or affirm) that the evidence you shall give to the court and jury in this trial, between the State and the prisoner at the bar, shall be the truth, the whole truth, and nothing but the truth; so help you, God.

Witness in a Criminal Action

You swear (or affirm) that the evidence you shall give to the court and jury in this action between the State and A. B. shall be the truth, the whole truth, and nothing but the truth; so help you, God.

Witness in Civil Cases

You swear (or affirm) that the evidence you shall give to the court and jury in this cause now on trial, wherein A. B. is plaintiff and C. D. defendant, shall be the truth, the whole truth, and nothing but the truth; so help you, God.

Witness to Prove a Will

You swear (or affirm) that you saw C. D. execute (or heard him acknowledge the execution of) this writing as his last will and testament; that you attested it in his presence and at his request; and that at the time of its execution (or at the time the execution was acknowledged) he was, in your opinion, of sound mind and disposing memory; so help you, God.

Witness before a Legislative Committee or Commission

You swear (or affirm) that the testimony you shall give to the committee (or commission) shall be the truth, the whole truth, and nothing but the truth; so help you, God.

General Oath

Any officer of the State or of any county or township, the term of whose oath is not given above, shall take an oath in the following form:

I, A. B., do swear (or affirm) that I will well and truly execute the duties of the office of ____ according to the best of my skill and ability, according to law; so help me, God. (R.C., c. 76, s. 6; 1874-5, c. 58, s. 2; Code, ss. 3057, 3315; 1903, c. 604; Rev., s. 2360; C.S., s. 3199; 1947, c. 71; 1959, c. 879, s. 5; 1967, c. 218, s. 2; 1969, c. 1190, ss. 50, 51; 1971, c. 381, s. 11; 1977, c. 344, s. 3; 1989 (Reg. Sess., 1990), c. 953; 1995, c. 379, s. 10; 1997-14, s. 1; 2011-284, s. 8; 2013-164, s. 2.)

Chapter 12.

Statutory Construction.

§ 12-1. Repealed by Session Laws 1957, c. 783, s. 3.

§12-2. Repeal of statute not to affect actions.

The repeal of a statute shall not affect any action brought before the repeal, for any forfeitures incurred, or for the recovery of any rights accruing under such statute. (1830, c. 44; R.C., c. 108, s. 1; 1879, c. 163; 1881, c. 48; Code, s. 3764; Rev., s. 2830; C.S., s. 3948.)

§ 12-3. Rules for construction of statutes.

In the construction of all statutes the following rules shall be observed, unless such construction would be inconsistent with the manifest intent of the General Assembly, or repugnant to the context of the same statute, that is to say:

(1)   Singular and Plural Number, Masculine Gender, etc. - Every word importing the singular number only shall extend and be applied to several persons or things, as well as to one person or thing; and every word importing the plural number only shall extend and be applied to one person or thing, as well as to several persons or things; and every word importing the masculine gender only shall extend and be applied to females as well as to males, unless the context clearly shows to the contrary.

(2)   Authority, to Three or More Exercised by Majority. - All words purporting to give a joint authority to three or more public officers or other persons shall be construed as giving such authority to a majority of such officers or other persons, unless it shall be otherwise expressly declared in the law giving the authority.

(3)   "Month" and "Year". - The word "month" shall be construed to mean a calendar month, unless otherwise expressed; and the word "year," a calendar year, unless otherwise expressed; and the word "year" alone shall be equivalent to the expression "year of our Lord." When a statute refers to a period of one or more months and the last month does not have a date corresponding to the initial date, the period shall expire on the last day of the last month.

(4)   Leap Year, How Counted. - In every leap year the increasing day and the day before, in all legal proceedings, shall be counted as one day.

(5)   "Oath" and "Sworn". - The word "oath" shall be construed to include "affirmation," in all cases where by law an affirmation may be substituted for an

oath, and in like cases the word "sworn" shall be construed to include the word "affirmed."

(6) "Person" and "Property". - The word "person" shall extend and be applied to bodies politic and corporate, as well as to individuals, unless the context clearly shows to the contrary. The words "real property" shall be coextensive with lands, tenements and hereditaments. The words "personal property" shall include moneys, goods, chattels, choses in action and evidences of debt, including all things capable of ownership, not descendable to heirs at law. The word "property" shall include all property, both real and personal.

(7) "Preceding" and "Following". - The words "preceding" and "following," when used by way of reference to any section of a statute, shall be construed to mean the section next preceding or next following that in which such reference is made; unless when some other section is expressly designated in such reference.

(8) "Seal". - In all cases in which the seal of any court or public office shall be required by law to be affixed to any paper issuing from such court or office, the word "seal" shall be construed to include an impression of such official seal, made upon the paper alone, as well as an impression made by means of a wafer or of wax affixed thereto.

(9) "Will". - The term "will" shall be construed to include codicils as well as wills.

(10) "Written" and "in Writing". - The words "written" and "in writing" may be construed to include printing, engraving, lithographing, and any other mode of representing words and letters: Provided, that in all cases where a written signature is required by law, the same shall be in a proper handwriting, or in a proper mark.

(11) "State" and "United States". - The word "state," when applied to the different parts of the United States, shall be construed to extend to and include the District of Columbia and the several territories, so called; and the words "United States" shall be construed to include the said district and territories and all dependencies.

(12) "Imprisonment for One Month," How Construed. - The words "imprisonment for one month," wherever used in any of the statutes, shall be construed to mean "imprisonment for thirty days."

(13) "Governor," "Senator," "Solicitor," "Elector," "Executor," "Administrator," "Collector," "Juror," and "Auditor". - The words "Governor," "Senator," "district attorney," "elector," "executor," "administrator," "collector," "juror," "auditor," and any other words of like character shall when applied to the holder of such office, or occupant of such position, be words of common gender, and they shall be a sufficient designation of the person holding such office or position, whether the holder be a man or woman.

(14) "Devisee" and "Devise". - The word "devisee," wherever used in any of the statutes, shall be construed to mean "devisee" as defined in G.S. 28A-1-1. The word "devise," wherever used in any of the statutes as a noun, shall be construed to mean a testamentary disposition of real or personal property and, wherever used in any of the statutes as a verb, shall be construed to mean to dispose of real or personal property by will.

(15) Requirement to consult with a committee or commission of the General Assembly. - All words purporting to require an individual or other entity to consult with a committee or commission of the General Assembly before taking an action shall be construed to require the entity to do all of the following:

a. Submit a report of the action under consideration to the chairs and staff of the committee or commission. The report shall include all information required by statute and the rules of that committee or commission. The staff of the committee or commission shall make the report available electronically to the members of the committee or commission and to the public.

b. Appear at a meeting of the committee or commission at which the matter is heard. Unless another period of time is specified by statute, the requirement to appear is satisfied if the committee or commission does not have a meeting at which the matter is heard within 90 days of receiving the required submission. (21 Hen. III; R.S., c. 31, s. 113; R.C., c. 31, s. 108; c. 108; Code, s. 3765; Rev., s. 2831; C.S., s. 3949; 1921, c. 30; 1973, c. 47, s. 2; 1977, c. 446, s. 4; 2011-284, s. 1; 2012-142, s. 6.11.)

§ 12-3.1. Fees and charges by agencies.

(a) Authority. - Only the General Assembly has the power to authorize an agency to establish or increase a fee or charge for the rendering of any service or fulfilling of any duty to the public. In the construction of a statute, unless that construction would be inconsistent with the manifest intent of the General Assembly or repugnant to the context of the statute, the legislative grant of authority to an agency to adopt rules shall not be construed as a grant of authority to the agency to establish by rule a fee or a charge for the rendering of any service or fulfilling of any duty to the public, unless the statute expressly provides for the grant of authority to establish a fee or charge for that specific service. Notwithstanding any other law, a rule adopted by an agency to establish or increase a fee or charge shall not go into effect until the agency has consulted with the Joint Legislative Commission on Governmental Operations on the amount and purpose of the fee or charge to be established or increased. The agency shall submit a request for consultation to all members of the Commission, the Commission Assistant, and the Fiscal Research Division of the General Assembly on the same date the notice of text of the rule is published. The request for consultation shall consist of a written report stating (i) the amount of the current fee or charge, if applicable, (ii) the amount of the proposed new or increased fee or charge, (iii) the statutory authority for the fee or charge, and (iv) a detailed explanation of the need for the establishment or increase of the fee or charge.

(a1)   If the Commission does not hold a meeting to hear the consultation required by subsection (a) of this section within 90 days after the notice of text of the rule has been published and the consultation request required by subsection (a) of this section has been submitted, the consultation requirement is satisfied.

(b)   Definitions. - The following definitions apply in this section:

(1)   Agency. - Every agency, institution, board, commission, bureau, department, division, council, member of the Council of State, or officer of the legislative, executive or judicial branches of State government. The term does not include counties, cities, towns, villages, other municipal corporations or political subdivisions of the State or any agencies of these subdivisions, the University of North Carolina, community colleges, hospitals, county or city boards of education, other local public districts, units, or bodies of any kind, or private corporations created by act of the General Assembly.

(2)   Rule. - Every rule, regulation, ordinance, standard, and amendment thereto adopted by any agency, including rules and regulations regarding substantive matters, standards for products, procedural rules for complying with statutory or regulatory authority or requirements and executive orders of the Governor.

(c) Exceptions. - This section does not apply to any of the following:

(1) Rules establishing fees or charges to State, federal or local governmental units.

(2) A reasonable fee or charge for copying, transcripts of public hearings, State publications, or mailing a document or other item.

(3) Reasonable registration fees covering the cost of a conference or workshop.

(4) Reasonable user fees covering the cost of providing data processing services.

(d) In lieu of the requirements of subsections (a) and (a1) of this section, the North Carolina State Ports Authority shall report the establishment or increase of any fee to the Joint Legislative Commission on Governmental Operations as provided in G.S. 136-262(a)(11). (1979, c. 559, s. 1; 1981, c. 695, ss. 1, 2; 1987, c. 564, s. 35; 1991, c. 418, s. 6; 2001-427, s. 8(a); 2002-99, s. 7(c); 2005-276, s. 6.8(b); 2011-145, s. 14.6(k).)

§ 12-4. Construction of amended statute.

Where a part of a statute is amended it is not to be considered as having been repealed and reenacted in the amended form; but the portions which are not altered are to be considered as having been the law since their enactment, and the new provisions as having been enacted at the time of the amendment.

Whenever the General Assembly (i) enacts a bill which purports to amend an existing general statute by deleting, adding, or substituting specific words or figures, and (ii) such bill also purports to set out the wording of the amended statute, or a portion thereof, as it will read after the amendment is accomplished, and (iii) there is a variance between the latter and the former, then, in such case, the latter shall control and be presumed to express the amendatory intent of the General Assembly. (1868-9, c. 270, s. 22; 1870-1, c. 111; Code, s. 3766; Rev., s. 2832; C.S., s. 3950; 1971, c. 115.)

Chapter 13.

Citizenship Restored.

§ 13-1. Restoration of citizenship.

Any person convicted of a crime, whereby the rights of citizenship are forfeited, shall have such rights automatically restored upon the occurrence of any one of the following conditions:

(1) The unconditional discharge of an inmate, of a probationer, or of a parolee by the agency of the State having jurisdiction of that person or of a defendant under a suspended sentence by the court.

(2) The unconditional pardon of the offender.

(3) The satisfaction by the offender of all conditions of a conditional pardon.

(4) With regard to any person convicted of a crime against the United States, the unconditional discharge of such person by the agency of the United States having jurisdiction of such person, the unconditional pardon of such person or the satisfaction by such person of a conditional pardon.

(5) With regard to any person convicted of a crime in another state, the unconditional discharge of such person by the agency of that state having jurisdiction of such person, the unconditional pardon of such person or the satisfaction by such person of a conditional pardon. (1971, c. 902; 1973, c. 251; c. 1262, s. 10; 1977, c. 813, s. 1; 1991, c. 274, s. 1; 2011-145, s. 19.1(h); 2012-83, s. 18; 2013-410, s. 2.)

§ 13-2. Issuance and filing of certificate or order of restoration.

(a) The agency, department, or court having jurisdiction over the inmate, probationer, parolee or defendant at the time his rights of citizenship are restored under the provisions of G.S. 13-1(1) shall immediately issue a certificate or order in duplicate evidencing the offender's unconditional discharge and specifying the restoration of his rights of citizenship.

The original of such certificate or order shall be promptly transmitted to the clerk of the General Court of Justice in the county where the official record of the case from which the conviction arose is filed. The clerk shall then file the certificate or order without charge with the official record of the case.

(b) In the case of a person convicted of a crime against another state or the United States, whose rights to citizenship have been restored according to G.S. 13-1, the following provisions shall apply:

(1) It shall be the duty of the clerk of the court in the county where such person resides, upon a showing by such person or his representative that the conditions of G.S. 13-1 have been met, to issue the certificate evidencing the offender's unconditional discharge and specifying the restoration of his rights of citizenship. For purposes of this subsection, the fulfillment of the conditions of G.S. 13-1 shall be considered met upon the presentation to the clerk of any paper writing from the agency of any other state or of the United States which had jurisdiction over such person, which shows that the conditions of G.S. 13-1 have been met.

(2) The certificate described in subdivision (b)(1) shall be filed by the clerk of the General Court of Justice in the county in which such person resides.

The provisions of this subsection apply equally to conditional and unconditional pardons by the governor of any other state or by the President of the United States, as well as unconditional discharges by the agency of another state or of the United States having jurisdiction over said person. (1971, c. 902; 1973, c. 251; 1977, c. 813, s. 2; 1991, c. 274, s. 2.)

§ 13-3. Issuance, service and filing of warrant of unconditional pardon.

In the event the rights of citizenship are restored by an unconditional pardon as specified in G.S. 13-1(2), the Governor, under the provisions of G.S. 147-23, shall issue his warrant therefor specifying the restoration of rights of citizenship to the offender; and the officer to whom the Governor issues his warrant to effect the release of the offender shall deliver a copy of the warrant to the offender under the provisions of G.S. 147-25. The original warrant bearing the officer's return as specified in G.S. 147-25 shall be filed by the clerk of the General Court of Justice without charge in the county where the official record of the case from which the conviction arose is filed. (1971, c. 902; 1973, c. 251.)

§ 13-4. Endorsement of warrant, service and filing of conditional pardon.

When the offender has satisfied all of the conditions of a conditional pardon, and his rights of citizenship have been restored under the provisions of G.S. 13-1(3), the Governor shall issue an endorsement to the original warrant which specified the conditions of the pardon. Such endorsement shall acknowledge that the offender has satisfied all of the conditions of the pardon.

The Governor shall then deliver the endorsement to the officer specified in G.S. 147-25 for service and delivery to the clerk. Service and delivery to the clerk and filing by the clerk shall be done in accordance with the provisions of G.S. 13-3 so that the endorsement reflecting satisfaction of all conditions of the pardon will be served and recorded as if it were a warrant of unconditional pardon. (1973, c. 251.)

§§ 13-5 through 13-10. Repealed by Session Laws 1971, c. 902.

Vision Books Order Form

Fax Orders: 1-980-299-5965

Phone Orders: 1-704-898-0770

E-mail Orders: www.visionbooks.org

Mail Orders: Vision Books, LLC
P.O. Box 42406
Charlotte, NC 28215

Shipp To:
Name_____
Address_____
City_____State_____Zip_____
Phone_____Fax_____
Email_____@_____

Bill To: We can bill a third party on your behalf.
Name_____
Address_____
City_____State_____Zip_____
Phone____(_____)_____Fax_____
Email_____@_____

Pamphlet Number ($15.00 Each)	Qty	Total Cost
_____	_____	_____
_____	_____	_____
_____	_____	_____
_____	_____	_____
_____	_____	_____
_____	_____	_____
_____	_____	_____
Full Volume Set 1-92	92 Pamphlets	1,380.00

Free Shipping Shipping & Handling on Full Volume Orders
Add $1.00 Shipping & Handling per pamphlet $_____

Total Cost $_____

Thank You for Your Support. Management!

DID YOU ENJOY THIS BOOK?

Vision Books, LLC would like to hear from you! If you or someone you know has been fasely imprisoned, we would like to hear your story. If the 'North Carolina Criminal Law and Procedure' has had an effect in your life or if you have suggestions, we would like to hear from you. Send your letters to:

Vision Books, LLC
Attn: Staff Writers
P.O. Box 42406
Charlotte, NC 28215
Email: staff@visionbooks.org

Order Additional Copies:

Fax Orders: 1-980-299-5965

Phone Orders: 1-704-898-0770

E-mail Orders: www.visionbooks.org

Mail Orders: Vision Books, LLC
                       P.O. Box 42406
                       Charlotte, NC 28215

www.ingramcontent.com/pod-product-compliance
Lightning Source LLC
Chambersburg PA
CBHW071423170526
45165CB00001B/371